I0010926

A guide to
ISTQB®
Foundation Certificate

A guide to
ISTQB®
Foundation Certificate

Based on latest ISTQB Foundation 2018 Syllabus

This book comes with video based tutorials support for each topic

Neeraj Kumar Singh

White Falcon
Publishing
www.whitefalconpublishing.com

A guide to ISTQB® Foundation Certification
Neeraj Kumar Singh

www.whitefalconpublishing.com

All rights reserved
First Edition, 2020
© Neeraj Kumar Singh, 2020
Cover design by White Falcon Publishing, 2020
Cover image source freepik.com
Interior images by Neeraj Kumar Singh

No part of this publication may be reproduced, or stored in a retrieval system,
or transmitted in any form by means of electronic, mechanical, photocopying or
otherwise, without prior written permission from the author.

The contents of this book have been certified and timestamped on the POA Network
blockchain as a permanent proof of existence. Scan the QR code or visit the URL
given on the back cover to verify the blockchain certification for this book.

Requests for permission should be addressed to
neerajsinghqa@gmail.com

ISBN - 978-93-89932-90-4

Disclaimer

Although all efforts have been made to ensure the uniqueness and accuracy of the contents of this book, the terminologies and practices may vary from organization to organizations. The definitions used here inline with the ISTQB® standard syllabus to meet the requirements of passing the exam.

I would like to acknowledge that this book relies heavily on the ISTQB® Foundation syllabus and standard glossary of terms used in software testing. In some cases, certain phrases were used verbatim to ensure the content adheres to the syllabus and glossary. Thus, the standard definition and terminologies are specific to ISTQB® standards to avoid any deviation.

Table of Contents

Preface

This book is written to assist the aspirants appearing or preparing for ISTQB® Foundation (CTFL) examination which will be conducted by International Software Testing Qualification Board (ISTQB®).

This book is being written in consent to assist the reader to understand various aspects of ISTQB® Foundation examination. It addresses the required understanding of testing terminologies, principles, practices, techniques, etc to understand and answer the questions in the examination.

Being first of its kind the book comes with supporting video tutorials of each topic to understand them in nutshell and learner quickly understand the topic.

This book is written considering 10 years of practical corporate training experience on ISTQB® Foundation preparation for various freshers and corporates. Thus, the pattern of the book will enable a reader to understand the content themselves and also get answers of common issues/queries arising while reading and understanding the book.

ALL THE BEST !!!

About the Examination

Learning Objectives/Level of Knowledge

Learning objectives are indicated for each section in this syllabus and classified as follows:

- **K1: Remember** – One need to know the definition and must know the meaning of it.
- **K2: Understand** – These topics requires details and process flow understanding.
- **K3: Apply** – These are for test design techniques to apply the steps and derive the answer.

All terms listed under "Terms" just below the chapter headings shall be remembered (K1) even if not explicitly mentioned in the details.

The examination will be based on ISTQB® standard syllabus given online on www.istqb.org

It includes 40 multiple choice questions. Each question having 4 options out of which only one can be right answer.

There is a time limit of 60 minutes to answer them all (Additional time for some special cases like language other than English)

There is no negative marking for ISTQB® Foundation certification examination.

Also, it's important for participants to remember that the K levels are marked for each topic to assist you prepare accordingly on each topic. So, kindly stick to it from certification point of view. What I mean to say is don't spend your time digging out details on a topic with K1 where you need to do the same with K3.

Chapter 1

Fundamentals of Testing

1. Fundamentals of Testing

Terms: Coverage, Debugging, Defect, Error, Failure, Quality, Quality assurance, Root cause, Test analysis, Test basis, Test case, Test completion, Test condition, Test control, Test data, Test design, Test execution, Test execution schedule, Test implementation, Test monitoring, Test object, Test objective, Test oracle, Test planning, Test procedure, Test suite, Testing, Testware, Traceability, Validation, Verification.

1.1. What is testing?

1.1.1. Introduction

A common perception of testing is that it only consists of running tests, i.e. executing the software. This is part of testing, but not all of the testing activities.

There are several other activities which are performed before and after test execution. These activities include:

> Planning and control, choosing test conditions, designing and executing test cases, checking results, evaluating exit criteria, reporting on the testing process and system under test, finalizing or completing closure activities after testing phase is completed

Testing also includes reviewing documents (including source code) and conducting static analysis.

Both dynamic testing and static testing can be used as a means for achieving similar objectives and will provide information that can be used to improve both the system being tested and the development and testing processes.

STATIC TESTING: Testing of a code, design or documents before using them as a reference to test the software. The process of conducting static testing is called as **Review**

DYNAMIC TESTING: Testing that involves the interaction and execution of the software of a component or system. Dynamic testing is performed with help of **Levels of testing**

Testing can have the following major objectives:

- Finding defects
- Gaining confidence about the level of quality
- Providing information for decision-making
- Preventing defects

These are the common objectives of testing but not limited to it. Depending on different factors we can add more to the typical objectives of testing. This includes

- To evaluate work products such as requirements, user stories, design, and code
- To verify whether all specified requirements have been fulfilled
- To validate whether the test object is complete and works as the users and other stakeholders expect
- To reduce the level of risk of inadequate software quality (e.g., previously undetected failures occurring in operation)
- To comply with contractual, legal, or regulatory requirements or standards, and/or to verify the test object's compliance with such requirements or standards

If considered further, testing objectives may vary depending upon the context of test level and development model in use. For example:

- During component testing, one objective may be to find as many failures as possible so that the underlying defects are identified and fixed early. Another objective may be to increase code coverage of the component tests.
- During acceptance testing, one objective may be to confirm that the system works as expected and satisfies requirements. Another objective of this testing may be to give information to stakeholders about the risk of releasing the system at a given time

The thought process and activities involved in designing tests early in the life cycle (verifying the test basis via test design) can help to prevent defects from being introduced into code.

Reviews of documents (e.g., requirements) and the identification and resolution of issues also help to prevent defects appearing in the code.

1.1.2. Testing and Debugging

Testing and debugging are different
TESTING: Testing or Dynamic Testing is a process where a tester experiences failures as a result of execution of tests and reports it to management and developer about the discrepancy in form of a defect. It doesn't deal with finding the root cause or fixing it. Usually performed by a Tester
DEBUGGING: It follows testing, where debugging deals with analysing, finding the root cause and removing the causes of failures in software. Generally performed by developer.

- Dynamic testing can show failures that are caused by defects.
- Debugging is the activity that finds, analyses and removes the cause of the failure.

The responsibility for each of these activities is usually testers tests and developers debug.

1.2. Why is Testing Necessary

In the technological age we live, work and play in software systems form an integral part of our lives. Think about it, everything from our cars to our coffee machines.

Software systems have simplified the way in which we bank, pay accounts and even shop.

When software works the way, it should and is supposed to, it makes our lives convenient. However, when software that does not work and does not do what it is supposed to do, it can be a more serious than just a source of inconvenience. It can cost companies to lose billions of dollars, even result in them being shut down or can claim human lives.

Let's look at a few actual scenarios to fully appreciate this concept:

China Airlines Airbus A300 crashing due to a software bug on April 26, 1994 killing 264 innocent lives

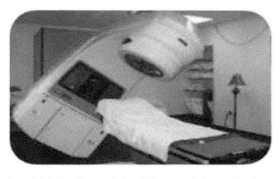

In 1985, Canada's Therac-25 radiation therapy machine malfunctioned due to software bug and delivered lethal radiation doses to patients, leaving 3 people dead and critically injuring 3 others

In April of 1999, a software bug caused the failure of a $1.2 billion military satellite launch, the costliest accident in history

In May of 1996, a software bug caused the bank accounts of 823 customers of a major U.S. bank to be credited with 920 million US dollars

As you can see, software bugs can be very expensive or even worse dangerous.

1.2.1. Testing's Contribution to Success.

It's common for software and system to be delivered into operation and, due to the presence of defects, to cause failures or otherwise not meet the customer needs. It's not that the product is not tested efficiently whereas at any point of time it's difficult to state that you have found all defects. As we can't conduct such unrealistic extent of testing, it's important to use appropriate techniques, which can help reduce the frequency of such problematic deliveries. These techniques can also help prevent defects from being introduced into the system.

There are several ways by which these techniques can be implemented:

- Having testers involved in requirements reviews or user story refinement could detect defects in these work products. The identification and removal of requirements defects reduces the risk of incorrect or untestable functionality being developed.
- Having testers work closely with system designers while the system is being designed can increase each party's understanding of the design and how to test it. This increased understanding can reduce the risk of fundamental design defects and enable tests to be identified at an early stage.
- Having testers work closely with developers while the code is under development can increase each party's understanding of the code and how to test it. This increased understanding can reduce the risk of defects within the code and the tests.
- Having testers verify and validate the software prior to release can detect failures that might otherwise have been missed, and support the process of removing the defects that caused the failures (i.e., debugging). This increases the likelihood that the software meets stakeholder needs and satisfies requirements.

1.2.2. Quality Assurance and Quality Control

Let's talk about Testing and Quality first. Regarding these two words, I always experience people getting confused to define the relation between them. Now, let me put it in a better way-

> *Testing is Quality oriented process or let's say it as Testing is a process by which you improve the quality of the system or software under test.*

I guess it stands to a reason that the more meaningful defects we find during testing, which means the more meaningful faults are fixed and thus less meaningful defects are found in production, therefore the greater our confidence in the Quality of the software is. Simple right ☺

Testing and Quality have the following relations:

- Testing can measure the quality of software
- Testing can give confidence in the quality of software
- Testing can improve the quality of future software

QUALITY: The degree to which a component, system or process meets specified requirements and/or user/customer needs and expectations

When it comes to understanding between testing and quality all we can say is testing is a quality-oriented process. By testing a product or system we enhance its quality. Here, defining or enhance the quality in product is not limited to finding defects and fixing them. When we understand the term quality there are many other terms which comes into consideration, where two common terms are Quality Assurance (QA) and Quality Control (QC).

Quality assurance is typically focused on adherence to proper processes, in order to provide confidence that the appropriate levels of quality will be achieved. When processes are carried out properly, the work products created by those processes are generally of higher quality, which contributes to defect prevention. In addition, the use of root cause analysis to detect and remove the causes of defects, along with the proper application of the findings of retrospective meetings to improve processes, are important for effective quality assurance.

Quality control involves various activities, including test activities, that support the achievement of appropriate levels of quality. Test activities are part of the overall software development or maintenance process.

1.2.3. Error, Defects and Failure

As per the syllabus and real-time scenarios there are various reasons which can cause a defect in your system. Some of the possibilities are unclear requirements, time pressure, complex code, complexity of infrastructure, changing technologies or many system interactions.

These are not limited to software, there are other causes in it comes to hardware. For example, Radiation, Magnetism, Electronic fields and pollutions can cause faults in firmware or influence the execution of software by changing the hardware conditions.

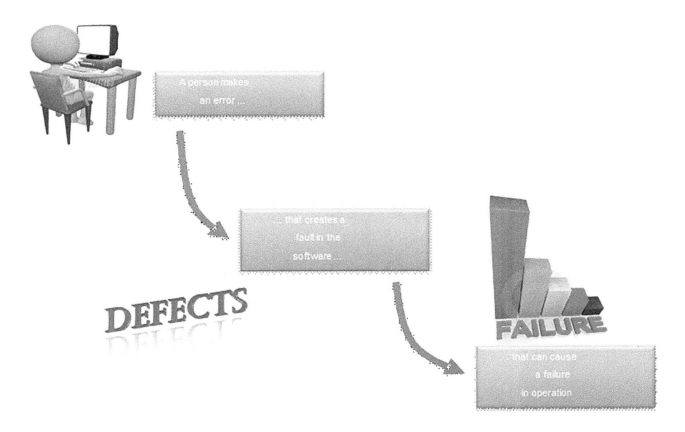

At this point let's understand that defects are not just because of code, this may occur due to unclear and incomplete specification, design or misunderstanding of the team as well.

We all know the pressure of strained timelines, of limited documentation, of just only knowing what you know at a given point in time. For these and a good few other reason, human beings make mistakes, we make errors.

ERROR(MISTAKE): A human action that produces a wrong result.

The results of the mistakes and errors we make, are the defects that we produce in specification documentation or in program code.

When a defect is executed and the system fails to do what it's supposed to or something that it shouldn't, this is called a failure.

FAULT(BUG, DEFECT) - A flaw in a component or system that can cause that component or system to fail to perform its required function.

FAILURE – The approach of executing a test and identifying a deviation. It's experienced by a tester when a test is executed and the result is different from the expected.

1.2.4. Defects, Root Causes and Effects

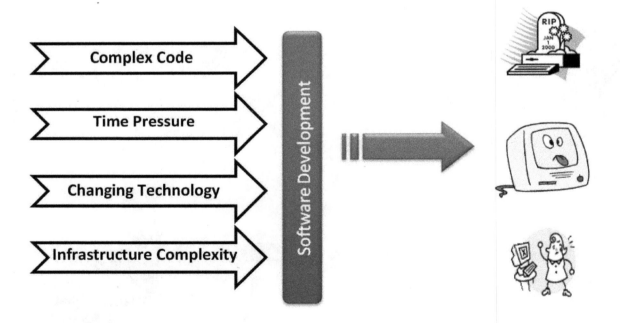

These causes can't be eliminated completely as we agree to the fact that we humans are error prone. But, can be minimized to a certain extent by taking some preventive measures like documenting clear specification, avoiding mistake at requirement gathering and design phase. Also, the process of reviewing them can be an added advantage to minimize defects at an initial level. Regarding review we will discuss more in chapter 3 of this syllabus.

Not all defects result in failure, sometimes the condition under which a piece of code needs to be executed never is, and thus a failure never occurs. Sometimes, its also just the misunderstanding of the scenario. Thus, its recommended that a evaluation of each work product by a senior team member is performed, before the document or source being used or referred further in process.

ROOT CAUSE - A source of a defect such that if it is removed, the occurrence of the defect type is decreased or removed.

WORK PRODUCT - A source document, code, design or resulting outcomes of any step in the entire process is called as work product.

1.3. Seven Testing Principles

These are some standard testing principles recommended after decades of testing practices and well proven, if followed. Let's understand some important concepts required to learn about principles.

EXHAUSTIVE TESTING: A test approach in which the test suite comprises of all possible combinations of input values and preconditions

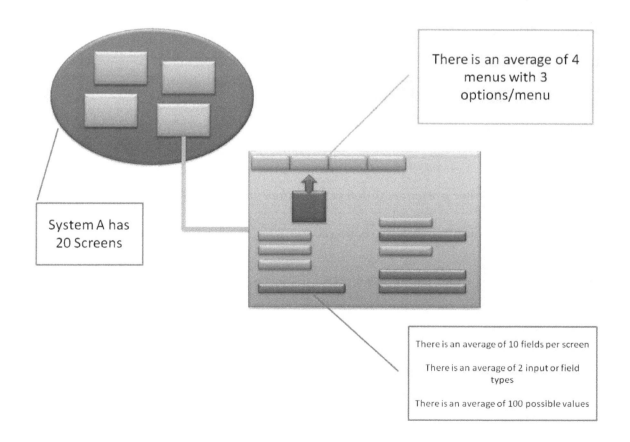

If we had to test everything:

The total number of tests required is:

$$20 \times 4 \times 3 \times 10 \times 2 \times 100 = 480\ 000$$

Let's say we could execute 1 test per second.

The total amount of time require = 480 000 seconds = 8 000 minutes = 133 hours = 17.7 days

If we took:

10 seconds per test, we would need 34 weeks

1 minute per test, we would need 4 years

10 minutes per test, we would need 40 years

As you can see, testing every possible combination can take years or even a lifetime to execute.

There is also a possibility that most tests would be duplicates and would prove nothing different from a set of tests that were derived using exhaustive testing.

The following 7 testing principles are covered in the ISTQB® foundation syllabus:

Principle 1	• Testing shows presence of defects, not absence
Principle 2	• Exhaustive testing is impossible
Principle 3	• Early testing saves time and money
Principle 4	• Defect cluster together
Principle 5	• Beware of Pesticide paradox
Principle 6	• Testing is context dependent
Principle 7	• Absence-of-errors is a fallacy

Let's explore each of these testing principles in more detail.

Principle 1 – Testing shows presence of defects, not their absence

- Testing is a process which helps to uncover defects but at any point of time we can't say that there are no defects.
- Irrespective of the results and execution done, we can't make a statement about no defects in the untested part of the application.
- Even if no defects are found, it is not a proof of correctness.

Principle 2 – Exhaustive testing is impossible

- Testing everything (all combinations of inputs and preconditions) is not feasible practically.

- As a result of this, test design techniques are being practiced to minimize the number of test cases with maximum coverage.
- Also, to avoid exhaustive testing, risk analysis and prioritization of test cases are used to focus on testing efforts with time constraints.

Principle 3 – Early testing saves time and money

- It's always cheaper to fix a defect earlier in lifecycle of development than later
- To understand this, imagine a defect found in testing phase which is due to an unclear requirement. Now to fix this defect we need to revise the requirement, redesign it followed by recode, to close the defect.
- Now from the above example we can say, if review of requirement was conducted at the time requirement gathering then we could have eliminated this at the same phase, saving time and cost both.

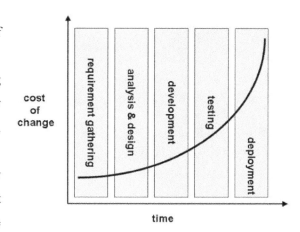

Principle 4 – Defect cluster together

- It's not mandatory that you find more defects in bigger modules compared to smaller. It can also be observed other way round.
- So, it's important that testing effort shall be focused proportionally to all modules irrespective of their size. Or more efforts to smaller and simple modules, where we usually go wrong because of over confidence.
- Sometime a small module contains a critical defect and is held responsible for most of the operational failures during pre-release.

Principle 5 – Beware of the Pesticide paradox

- It's a common practice among us that we try to execute a plan again and again assuming, it would work sometime. But, on the other side when you know, you couldn't score well in your exams based on the plan you defined, then it's obvious that you try to redefine your plan when you look at the exams of next year.
- Similarly, if the same tests are repeated over and over again, eventually the same set of test cases will no longer find any new defects.

- To overcome this "pesticide paradox", test cases need to be regularly reviewed and revised, and new and different tests need to be written to exercise different parts of the software or system to find potentially more and different defects.

Principle 6 – Testing is context dependent

- It's very simple for one to understand that a calculator and dial pad of phone are not developed or tested in same manner, though they look similar.
- Thus, the principle states - Testing is done differently for projects from different domain and contexts. For example, safety-critical software is tested differently from an e-commerce site.

Principle 7 – Absence-of-errors is a fallacy

- Last but not the least, testing and finding defects is all about meeting the requirements.
- Finding and fixing defects does not help if the system built is unusable and does not fulfil the users' needs and expectations.

1.4. Test Process

1.4.1. Test Process in Context

The most visible part of testing is test execution. But to be effective and efficient, test plans should also include time to be spent on planning the tests, designing test cases, preparing for execution and evaluating results.

Fundamental test process is also known as Software Testing Lifecycle (STLC). This cycle shows the end to end activities as part of testing phase.

Contextual factors that influence the test process for an organization, include, but are not limited to:

- Software development lifecycle model and project methodologies being used
- Test levels and test types being considered
- Product and project risks
- Business domain
- Operational constraints, including but not limited to:
  - o Budgets and resources
  - o Timescales
  - o Complexity
  - o Contractual and regulatory requirements
- Organizational policies and practices
- Required internal and external standards

1.4.2. Test Activities and Tasks

The fundamental test process consists of the following main activities:

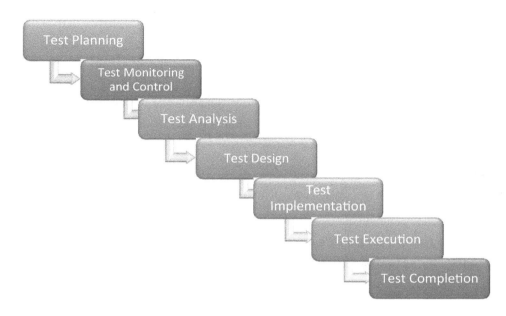

Although logically sequential, the activities in the process may overlap or take place concurrently. Tailoring these main activities within the context of the system and the project is usually required.

Test Planning

Test planning is the activity of defining the overall objectives of testing and specifying test activities in order to meet the objectives and mission.

Note: Test plan prepared initially can also be tweaked based on the feedback from monitoring and control activities. This is a responsibility of Test Manager.

Now, let's see what are the activities performed in **Test planning** phase:

- Defining the scope of testing.
- Determining the risks and identifying the objectives of testing.
- Defining the overall approach of testing, including the definition of the test levels.
- Defining the Entry and Exit criteria.
- Integrating and coordinating the testing activities into the software lifecycle activities.
- Making decisions about what to test, what roles will perform the test activities, how the test activities be done and how the test results be evaluated.
- Scheduling test analysis and design activities.
- Scheduling test implementation, execution and evaluation.
- Assigning resources for the different activities defined.
- Defining the amount, level of detail, structure and templates for the test documentation.

- Selecting metrics for monitoring and controlling test preparation and execution.

We will be learning this phase in more detail in Chapter 5. Rather, you will be required to get in depth of test planning from the examination point of view.

Test Monitoring and Control

Test monitoring involves the on-going comparison of actual progress against the test plan using any test monitoring metrics defined in the test plan. Test monitoring is generally defined as the process of measuring the progress on the project.

Test control is set of necessary actions which is defined in line with each planned activity. It involves taking actions necessary to meet the objectives of the test plan (which may be updated over time). These actions will be applied or implemented when we experience a deviation in the scheduled plan.

To decide when a Control action is necessary to be implemented, we keep monitoring the ongoing activity by comparing actual progress against the plan. This process of tracking and comparing is called as **Test Monitoring.**

- Test Monitoring is done with help of **Test Metrics**. It's a measure of progress of the project
- For example,

$$\text{Test Execution Rate} = \frac{\text{Total number test cases executed}}{\text{Total number of test cases palanned to execute}} \, x \, 100$$

A **Test Metrics** could be probably defined as certain calculation or combination which can help you measure an entity, activity or progress on any activity.

By using this metrics, we can evaluate the daily execution rate as monitoring activity. If a deviation is observed with respect to planned execution rate then the respective control action will be implemented to overcome the deviation.

Test Monitoring and control is consistent activity throughout the testing lifecycle as you never know when you can experience a deviation from the planned activities or desired quality to be achieved. In simple terms the activities can be listed as:

- Measuring the actual test results with those of expected and defined (Such as criteria, coverage, etc)
- Determining if we need to assist our efforts with more test cases to achieve significant coverage
- Implementing control actions if any deviations is observed

Test Analysis

Test analysis is the activity during which we start with understanding the requirements and general testing objectives are transformed into tangible test conditions and test cases.

TEST BASIS: All documents or work products, from which the requirements of a component or system can be analysed and understood. The documentation on which the test cases are based. If a document can be amended only by way of formal amendment procedure, then the test basis is called a frozen test basis.

The **test analysis** activity have the following major tasks:

- Reviewing the test basis such as:
  - o Requirements
  - o Risk analysis reports
  - o Architecture
  - o Design
  - o Interface specifications
- Evaluating testability of the test basis and test objects
- Evaluating the test basis and test items to identify defects of various types, such as:
  - o Ambiguities
  - o Omissions
  - o Inconsistencies
  - o Inaccuracies
  - o Contradictions
- Identifying and prioritizing **test conditions** based on analysis of test items, the specification, behaviour and structure of the software. (Test conditions are same as test scenario)

Test Design

During test design, the test conditions are elaborated into high-level test cases, sets of high-level test cases, and other *testware*. So, test analysis answers the question "what to test?" while test design answers the question "how to test?"

Test design includes the following major activities:

- Designing and prioritizing high level test cases
- Identifying necessary test data to support the test conditions and test cases
- Designing the test environment set-up and identifying any required infrastructure and tools
- Creating bi-directional traceability between test basis and test cases. Eg. Requirement Traceability Matrix.

TESTWARE: Artefacts produced during the test process required to plan, design, and execute tests, such as documentation, scripts, inputs, expected results, set-up and clear-up procedures, files, databases, environment, and any additional software or utilities used in testing.

TEST DATA: Any kind of input value to the application which assist your application or product testing.

Test Implementation

During test implementation, the testware necessary for test execution is created and/or completed, including sequencing the test cases into test procedures. So, test design answers the question "how to test?" while test implementation answers the question "do we now have everything in place to run the tests?"

Test implementation has the following major tasks:

- Developing and prioritizing test procedures, creating test data and, optionally, preparing test harnesses (stubs & drivers) and writing automated test scripts.
- Creating test suites from the test procedures for efficient test execution.
- Arranging the test suites within a test execution schedule in a way that results in efficient test execution.
- Verifying that the test environment has been set up correctly.
- Verifying and updating bi-directional traceability between the test basis and test cases.

TEST SUITE: Collection of test cases put together to be executed at once. This is also called as a test set in some of the test management tool.

TEST EXECUTION SCHEDULE: A test suite further arranged with respect to their dependency(Logical & Technical) and priority to determine the order of execution.

Test Execution

During test execution, test suites are executed in accordance with the test execution schedule. As a part of this phase all levels (unit, integration, system, non-functional, etc) of testing will be performed. It is often possible that the activities of Implementation and Execution phases may be combined as the execution may determine additional test cases, re-ordering, tweaking of environment and fulfilling any such necessary acts which we would have missed or misinterpreted earlier.

Test execution includes the following major activities:

- Executing tests either manually or by using test execution tools, according to the planned sequence.
- Logging the outcome of test execution and recording the identities and versions of the software under test, test tools and testware.
- Determining if additional test cases are required as a result of monitoring.
- Reporting discrepancies as incidents and analysing them in order to establish their cause (e.g., a defect in the code, in specified test data, in the test document, or a mistake in the way the test was executed).
- Repeating test activities as a result of action taken for each discrepancy, for example, re-execution of a test that previously failed in order to confirm a fix (confirmation testing/retesting), execution of a corrected test and/or execution of tests in order to ensure that defects have not been introduced in unchanged areas of the software or that defect fixing did not uncover other defects (regression testing).

Note: We will learn more on Entry and Exit criteria in Chapter 5.

All Power is within You!!

Test Completion

Test completion activities collect data from completed test activities to consolidate experience, testware, facts and figures. Test completion activities occur at project milestones such as when a software system is released, a test project is completed (or cancelled), a milestone has been achieved, or a maintenance release has been completed.

Test completion activities include the following major tasks:

- Checking which planned deliverables have been delivered
- Closing incident reports or raising change records for any that remain open
- Documenting the acceptance of the system
- Creating test summary report
- Finalizing and archiving testware, test environment and test infrastructure for later reuse
- Handing over the testware to the maintenance organization
- Analyzing lessons learned to determine changes needed for future releases and projects
- Using the information gathered to improve test maturity

1.4.3. Test Work Products

Work products are any such documentation which is prepared as part of an activity within a process. These documents could be an output of a phase and help as an input to the next phase. Also, can be called as a document which is created as part of the process and used to assist subsequent activities.

Test work products are created as part of the test process. Just as there is significant variation in the way that organizations implement the test process, there is also significant variation in the types of work products created during that process, in the ways those work products are organized and managed, and in the names used for those work products.

We may have different set of test work products within each phase. Its necessary to know, what these documents are and how helpful they can be.

Test Planning Work Products

During Test planning we create one or more test plans. The test plan includes information about the test basis, to which the other test work products will be related via traceability information as well as entry and exit criteria (or definition of done) which will be used during test monitoring and control and later within the entire lifecycle.

When we say one or more, it generally means, additional plans may include a backup plan or different plans for various levels, types of risk, addressing specific scenarios, test automation, etc.

Test Monitoring and Control Work Products

As we know about the monitoring activities, Test monitoring and control work products typically include various types of test reports, including test progress reports (produced on an ongoing and/or a regular basis) and test summary reports (produced at various completion milestones). All test reports should provide details about the test progress as of the date of the report, including summarizing the test execution results once those become available. These reports will be created with help of metrics and will be helpful for the test manager to determine the adequate control actions. Test monitoring and control work products should also address project management concerns, such as task completion, resource allocation and usage, and effort.

Test Analysis Work Products

As now we are familiar with the activities performed during test analysis, there are several outputs of these activities. Test analysis work products include

- The list of defined and prioritized test conditions
- Traceability document between test conditions and test basis
- Test charters in case of Exploratory testing
  Test analysis may also result in the discovery and reporting of defects in the test basis.

Test Design Work Products

Test design results in test cases and sets of test cases to exercise the test conditions defined in test analysis. It is often a good practice to design high-level test cases, without concrete values for input data and expected results.

Test design work products generally include

- Test cases (logical or concrete)
- Necessary test data
- The design of the test environment
- The details of infrastructure and tools
  Test case are also required to have a traceability between the test scenario and test basis respectively.

Test Implementation Work Products

Test implementation work products include:

- Test procedures and the sequencing of those test procedures
- Test suites
- A test execution schedule
- Test Scripts

Ideally, once test implementation is complete, achievement of coverage criteria established in the test plan can be demonstrated via bi-directional traceability between test procedures and specific elements of the test basis, through the test cases and test conditions.

Test Execution Work Products

Test execution generally incudes execution of test cases, documenting the outcomes and preparation of reports. Test execution work products include:

- Documentation of the status of individual test cases or test procedures (e.g., ready to run, pass, fail, blocked, deliberately skipped, etc.)
- Defect reports
- Documentation about which test item(s), test object(s), test tools, and testware were involved in the testing.
- Coverage measure reports

Test Completion Work Products

This phase includes activities related to test closure (retrospectives in case of agile). Test completion work products include

- Test summary reports,
- Action items for improvement of subsequent projects or iterations (e.g., following a project Agile retrospective)
- Change requests or product backlog items
- Finalized testware
- Acceptance report of the product
- Reports assisting the details of defect that remain open.

1.4.4. Traceability Between the Test Basis and Test Work Products

In order to implement effective test monitoring and control, it is important to establish and maintain traceability throughout the test process between each element of the test basis and the various test work products associated with that element, as described above. In addition to the evaluation of test coverage, good traceability supports:

- Analysing the impact of changes
- Making testing auditable
- Improving the understandability of test progress reports and test summary reports to include the status of elements of the test basis (e.g., requirements that passed their tests, requirements that failed their tests, and requirements that have pending tests)
- Relating the technical aspects of testing to stakeholders in terms that they can understand
- Providing information to assess product quality, process capability, and project progress against business goals
- To evaluate if we have missed any aspect to be tested or to be documented.

1.5. The Psychology of Testing

1.5.1. Introduction

The mindset to be used while testing and reviewing is different from that used while developing software. With the right mindset developers are able to test their own code, but separation of this responsibility to a tester is typically done to help focus effort and provide additional benefits, such as an independent view by trained and professional testing resources.

It becomes very important to keep the psychological aspects in consideration when working in mixed teams. Also, communication and reporting is equally important to be done effectively to keep the teams objectively oriented towards a common goal of the project.

1.5.2. Human Psychology and Testing

In this topic, we want you to know how independent a testing team can be within an organisation. As the history includes, the testing came into practice to create author bias and have people with different perspective evaluating a piece of code other than the one who created it.

The best example to understand this –

> *"A student writing a 3 hour long academic examination gets some time to revise the answer script before submission. No matter, what count of attempts you give to revision still there is possibility of missing few things which are wrong. But, when the same answer script is evaluated by a teacher, he/she can evaluate and point out the mistakes. As, the person evaluating was not involved in writing it."*

Considering this theory is best to understand the significance of independent testing being practiced but not limited to it. These are areas where independence degree may vary and include -

- Independent testing may be carried out at any level of testing.
- A certain degree of independence (avoiding the author bias) often makes the tester more effective at finding defects and failures.
- Independence is not, however, a replacement for familiarity, and developers can efficiently find many defects in their own code.

Identifying failures during testing may be perceived as criticism against the product and against the author. As a result, testing is often seen as a destructive activity, even though it is very constructive in the management of product risks.

Looking for failures in a system requires curiosity, professional pessimism, a critical eye, attention to detail, good communication with development peers, and experience on which to base error guessing.If errors, defects or failures are communicated in a constructive way, bad feelings between the testers and the analysts, designers and developers can be avoided. This applies to defects found during reviews as well as in testing.

The tester and test leader need good interpersonal skills to communicate factual information about defects, progress and risks in a constructive way. For the author of the software or document, defect information can help them improve their skills. Defects found and fixed during testing will save time and money later and reduce risks. Communication problems may occur, particularly if testers are seen only as messengers of unwanted news about defects.

However, there are several ways to improve communication and relationships between testers and others. Also, it is more important to keep these points in consideration when experiencing a mixed team of tester and developer and higher degree of Independence:

- Start with collaboration rather than battles – remind everyone of the common goal of better-quality systems
- Communicate findings on the product in a neutral, fact-focused way without criticizing the person who created it, for example, write objective and factual incident reports and review findings
- Try to understand how the other person feels and why they react as they do
- Confirm that the other person has understood what you have said and vice versa

1.5.3. Tester's and Developer's Mindset

Developers and testers often think differently. The primary objective of development is to design and build a product whereas, for test team, it is to evaluate the success of products. In simple terms, we may also say it as – *Developers are constructive in nature whereas, tester use a destructive nature.* As discussed earlier, the objectives of testing include verifying and validating the product, finding defects prior to release, and so forth. These are different sets of objectives which require different mindsets. Bringing these mindsets together helps to achieve a higher level of product quality.

But, sometimes, the different mindsets may lead to misunderstanding of an issue or fixing it. How? Being a developer, you think from a confirmation, constructive nature and whenever you look at your work, you have already a picture of what you have written where and why. But, when a tester (like a user) tries to work on it, having a different perception may find different defects. Now, what if a defect is identified and reported to developer and developer doesn't understand what's the issue all about. It would be time consuming, maximised effort and lot of rework required to close such issues.

That's where we recommend that developer should also posses a user perspective to help prevent defects or find defects at an early phase. This would not only save the time, but also, increase quality of the product, reduce rework and cost of overall quality and improve communications between development and testing team.

Quick Revision & Tips on Chapter 1

1. Remember what and why testing is important.
2. Quite often a question appears on objective of testing.
3. Remember the difference between Error, Defect (Fault) and Failure with example.
4. Understand what is difference between root cause and defect.
5. Question from principle of testing will generally be given with details of principle.
6. Principle of testing can also be asked as match the following.
7. It is important to remember the activities within each test phase. Generally asked as match the following.
8. Work products and traceability can be combined to ask a general question.
9. Psychology of testing would concentrate on the possibilities of conflict and how you can prevent gaps between team.
10. Mindset of developer would require an understanding of what additional knowledge and skill tester possess over developer and others teams.
11. Quite often the questions in this chapter include words like BEST, MOST, LIKELY which means all option would sound right, you have to pick the most relevant.
12. Quite often the question in this chapter includes word like NOT or FALSE which means you need to pick the irrelevant option from given.
13. Bulleted point covers maximum number of questions from this chapter.
14. This chapter will have 8 questions in the examination with following breakup.

Chapter 1 Question Distribution	K-Level	Number of Questions per LO	Suggested Points per question	
Keywords	K1	Exactly ONE question based on the definition of a keyword from Chapter 1	1	**There is a total of 8 questions required for Chapter 1.** **K1 = 2** **K2 = 6** **K3 = 0** **Number of points for this chapter = 8**
FL-1.1.1 FL-1.5.1	K1	Exactly ONE question based on either of these LOs is required.	1	
FL-1.1.2 FL-1.2.1 FL-1.2.2 FL-1.2.3 FL-1.2.4 FL-1.3.1 FL-1.4.1 FL-1.4.2 FL-1.4.3 FL-1.4.4 FL-1.5.2	K2	Exactly SIX questions based on this set of 11 LOs are required. Each question must cover a DIFFERENT LO.	1	

 # For the exact topic number please refer the ISTQB® official syllabus.

Sample Questions on Chapter 1

1. **Test planning has which of the following major tasks?**
   i. **Determining the scope and risks, and identifying the objectives of testing.**
   ii. **Determining the test approach (techniques, test items, coverage, identifying and interfacing the teams involved in testing, testware)**
   iii. **Reviewing the Test Basis (such as requirements, architecture, design, interface)**
   iv. **Determining the exit criteria.**
     a) i,ii,iv are true and iii is false
     b) i,,iv are true and ii is false
     c) i,ii are true and iii,iv are false
     d) ii,iii,iv are true and i is false

2. **Test Conditions are derived from:-**
   a) Specifications
   b) Test Cases
   c) Test Data
   d) Test Design

3. **Which of the following is a part of Test Completion?**
   i. **Checking which planned deliverables have been delivered**
   ii. **Defect report analysis.**
   iii. **Finalizing and archiving testware.**
   iv. **Analysing lessons.**
     a) i, ii, iv are true and iii is false
     b) i, ii, iii are true and iv is false
     c) i, iii, iv are true and ii is false
     d) All of above are true

4. **Consider the following statements about early test design:**
   i. **Early test design can prevent defect multiplication**
   ii. **Defects found during early test design are cheaper to fix**
   iii. **Early test design can't help find faults**
   iv. **Early test design can cause changes to the test environment**
   v. **Early test design takes more effort**
     a) i, & ii are true. Iii, iv & v are false
     b) iii is true, I, ii, iv & v are false
     c) iii & iv are true. i, ii & v are false
     d) i, iii, iv & v are true, ii us false

5. **The cost of fixing a defect:**
   a) Is not important
   b) Increases as we move the product towards live use
   c) Decreases as we move the product towards live use
   d) Is more expensive if found in requirements than functional design

6. **What is the main reason for testing software before releasing it?**
   a) To show that system will work after release
   b) To decide when the software is of sufficient quality to release
   c) To find as many bugs as possible before release
   d) To give information for a risk-based decision about release

7. **When reporting faults found to developers, testers should be:**
   a) As polite, constructive and helpful as possible
   b) Firm about insisting that a bug is not a "feature" if it should be fixed
   c) Diplomatic, sensitive to the way they may react to criticism
   d) All of the above

8. **Test cases are designed during:**
   a) Test planning
   b) Test design
   c) Test implementation.
   d) Test analysis

9. **As a result of risk analysis, more testing is being directed to those areas of the system under test where initial testing found more defects than average.**
   Which of the following testing principles is being applied?
   a) Beware of the pesticide paradox.
   b) Testing is context dependent.
   c) Absence-of-errors is a fallacy.
   d) Defects cluster together.

10. **Which of the following is MOST valid goal for a test team?**
    a) To determine whether enough component tests were executed within system testing
    b) To detect as many failures as possible so that defects can be identified and fixed
    c) To prove that all defects have been identified
    d) To prove that any remaining defect will not cause any failures

Answer to the questions can be found at the last page of the book

Chapter 2

Testing Throughout the Software Development Lifecycle

2. Testing Throughout the Software Development Life Cycle

Terms: Acceptance testing, Alpha testing, Beta testing, Black-box testing, Commercial off-the-shelf (COTS), Component integration testing, Component testing, Confirmation testing, Contractual acceptance testing, Functional testing, Impact analysis, Integration testing, Maintenance testing, Non-functional testing, Operational acceptance testing, Regression testing, Regulatory acceptance testing, Sequential Development model, System integration testing, System testing, Test level, Test object, Test objective, Test type, User acceptance testing, White-box testing

2.1. Software Development Lifecycle Models

Software development model is the entire process of making an application or product. This includes the main phases as requirement gathering, design, code, testing and maintenance. All the models require equal efforts and contribution from different team across the process.

We are aware of several Software Development Models from traditional approaches and recent approaches. At this point of time, let us understand that there are several other factors like efficient documentation, team collaboration and effective communication which help reduce both project cost and project risk by heading off misconceptions and oversights as early in the process as possible.

Test activities are related to software development activities. Different development life cycle models need different approaches to testing. In the sections that follow, we will review the Sequential and Iterative/ Incremental Development Models. Once we have understood the approach taken during these models, we will then look at how testing fits in.

2.1.1. V-model (Sequential Development Model)

It is an important part of a tester's role to be familiar with the common software development lifecycle models so that appropriate test activities can take place. In any software development lifecycle model, there are several characteristics of good testing:

* For every development activity, there is a corresponding test activity
* Each test level has test objectives specific to that level
* Test analysis and design for a given test level begin during the corresponding development activity
* Testers are involved in reviewing work products (e.g., requirements, design, user stories, etc.) as soon as drafts are available

Didn't understand what these means and how are they fit a development model? Let's understand V- Model first to understand these good characteristics of testing.

A common type of V-model uses four test levels, corresponding to the four development levels.

V MODEL: A framework to describe the software development lifecycle activities from requirements specification to maintenance. The V-model illustrates how testing activities can be integrated into each phase of the software development lifecycle.

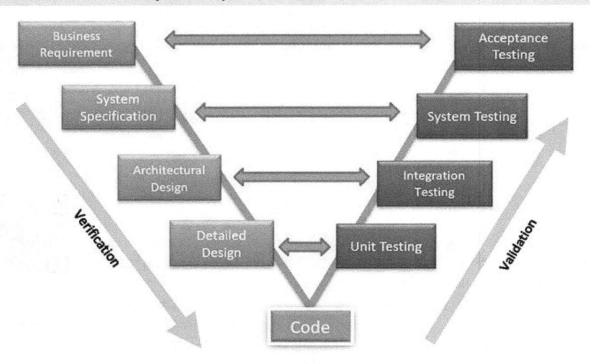

The four levels used in this syllabus are:

- Component (unit) testing
- Integration testing
- System testing
- Acceptance testing

In practice, a V-model may have more, fewer or different levels of development and testing, depending on the project and the software product. Also it varies from organisation to organisation.

> *For example, there may be component integration testing after component testing, and system integration testing after system testing.*

Software work products (such as business scenarios or use cases, requirements specifications, design documents and code) produced during development are often the basis of testing in one or more test levels.

Verification and validation (and early test design) can be carried out during the development of the software work products.

COMPONENT INTEGRATION TESTING: Component integration testing focuses on the interactions and interfaces between integrated components. Component integration testing is performed after component testing, and is generally automated.

SYSTEM INTEGRATION TESTING: System integration testing focuses on the interactions and interfaces between systems, packages, and microservices. System integration testing can also cover interactions with, and interfaces provided by, external organizations.

Verification	Validation
➢ Verification resembles that all the requirements of customer is covered or not is verified for completeness.	➢ Validation resembles that all the functionalities are correctly working or not is validated for correctness.
➢ Verification = process oriented.	➢ Validation = product oriented.
➢ Verification: is a QA process	➢ Validation: is QC process i.e. testing.
➢ Verification: make sure you have we build the product right.	➢ Validation: to make sure have we build the right product.
➢ Verification means checking a product/project manually by verifying the documents, reviewing the code and so on.	➢ Validation in the sense giving actual input's to the system and observing the outputs in all angles. This is final testing which has to go on very consciously.
➢ Product verification is a set of measures applied before the product is put to use to ensure that the intended features are built into the product.	➢ Validation is a (runtime) process when the user validates the product against the requirement and confirms that the product is valid for use.

2.1.2. Iterative-incremental Development Model

Iterative-incremental development is the process of establishing requirements, designing, building and testing a system, done as a series of shorter development cycles. Each iteration delivers working software which is a growing subset of the overall set of features until the final software is delivered or development is stopped.

Examples are:

- **Rational Unified Process** - Each iteration tends to be relatively long (e.g., two to three months), and the feature increments are correspondingly large, such as two or three groups of related features
- **Scrum** - Each iteration tends to be relatively short (e.g., hours, days, or a few weeks), and the feature increments are correspondingly small, such as a few enhancements and/or two or three new features
- **Kanban** - Implemented with or without fixed-length iterations, which can deliver either a single enhancement or feature upon completion, or can group features together to release at once
- **Spiral** - Involves creating experimental increments, some of which may be heavily re-worked or even abandoned in subsequent development work

The resulting system produced at the end of each iteration may be tested at several test levels during that iteration.

> NOTE: Agile is not a part of this syllabus, this is only for understanding the model.

Iterative-incremental Development Model Example:

We have decided to produce a system that will allow an organisation to capture and maintain invoices.
During iteration 1 we want to deliver the following functionality:

- Create/Maintain Base Interest Rates
- Create/Maintain Users
- Create/Maintain Client
- Work Flow Routing

During iteration 2 we want to deliver the following functionality:

- Create/Maintain Invoices

During iteration 2 we want to deliver the following functionality:

- Integration to GL
- Integration to Document generation, retrieval and delivery

It's important to understand that an increment, added to others developed previously, forms a growing partial system, which should also be tested.

> Regression testing is increasingly important on all iterations after the first one. Verification and validation can be carried out on each increment.

2.1.3. Testing within a Life Cycle Model

Now we know what V-Model and its corresponding activities are, let's understand in any life cycle model, there are several characteristics of good testing:

- For every **Development Activity** there is a corresponding **Testing Activity**
- Each test level has test **Objectives** specific to that level
- The **analysis and design** of tests for a given test level should begin during the corresponding development activity
- Testers should be involved in reviewing documents **as soon as drafts** are available in the development life cycle

Test levels can be combined or reorganized depending on the nature of the project or the system architecture.
For example, for the integration of a Commercial Off-The-Shelf (COTS) software product into a system, the purchaser may perform:

1. Integration testing at the system level
   - Integration to the infrastructure and other systems, or system deployment

2. Acceptance testing
   • Functional and/or non-functional, and user and/or operational testing

2.2. Test Levels

2.2.1. Introduction

For each of the test levels, the following can be identified:

• Generic objectives;
• Work product(s) being referenced for deriving test cases (i.e. the test basis);
• Test object (i.e. what is being tested);
• Typical defects and failures to be found;
• Test harness requirements and tool support; and
• Specific approaches and responsibilities.

Testing a system's configuration data shall be considered during test planning, if such data is part of a system.

2.2.2. Component Testing

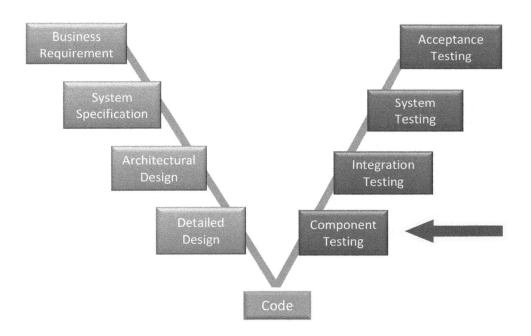

Earlier we looked at the V-Model. As part of the model, the level of test performed against the Detailed Design of the system is Component or Unit Testing. Let's explore this in more detail.

The generic test objective of Component testing (also known as unit, module, structure, code or program testing) is to test for defects in, and verify the functionality and behaviour of software modules, programs, objects, classes, etc., that are separately testable as units.

The other major objectives of component testing include:

- Reducing risk
- Verifying whether the functional and non-functional behaviours of the component are as designed and specified
- Building confidence in the component's quality
- Finding defects in the component · Preventing defects from escaping to higher test levels

Component testing may include testing of functionality and specific non-functional characteristics, such as resource-behaviour (e.g., searching for memory leaks) or robustness testing, as well as structural testing (e.g., decision coverage).

Typically, component testing occurs with access to the code being tested and with the support of a development environment, such as a unit test framework or debugging tool. In practice, component testing usually involves the programmer who wrote the code.

Defects are typically fixed as soon as they are found, without formally managing these defects.

One approach to component testing is to prepare and automate test cases before coding. This is called a test-first approach or test-driven development. This approach is discussed in Agile tester extension certification.

- *This approach is highly iterative and is based on cycles of developing test cases, then building and integrating small pieces of code, and executing the component tests correcting any issues and iterating until they pass.*

The **Test Basis** (Work product(s) being referenced for deriving test cases) for Component Testing are:

- Component requirements
- Detailed design
- Code

The typical **Test Objects** (i.e. what is being tested) for Component Testing are:

- Components
- Programs
- Data conversion / migration programs
- Database modules

And the typical **Defects and Failure** which can be identified with help of Component Testing are:

- Incorrect functionality (e.g., not as described in design specifications)
- Data flow problems
- Incorrect code and logic

COTS(Customer-Off-The-Self): These are external (3rd Party)software integrated with software under test. For Eg. An e-commerce website using a 3rd party payment gateway.

2.2.3. Integration Testing

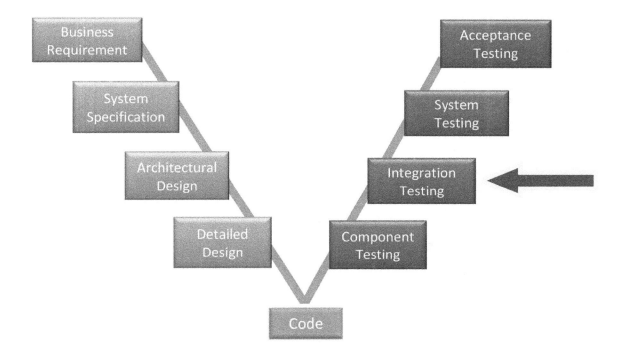

So, we started of our testing by verifying that the components of our system are functional.

During integration testing, we test interfaces between components, interactions with different parts of a system, such as the operating system, file system and hardware, and interfaces between systems. Here, integration can also be called as interfaces, interactions or data flow between modules, which all mean the same.

Objectives of integration testing include:

- Reducing risk
- Verifying whether the functional and non-functional behaviours of the interfaces are as designed and specified
- Building confidence in the quality of the interfaces
- Finding defects (which may be in the interfaces themselves or within the components or systems) Preventing defects from escaping to higher test levels

There may be more than one level of integration testing and it may be carried out on test objects of varying size as follows:

1. **Component integration testing** tests the interactions between software components and is done after component testing

2. **System integration testing** tests the interactions between different systems or between hardware and software and may be done after system testing. In this case, the developing organization may control only one side of the interface. This might be considered as a risk. This level is generally performed in following cases – Software-Software Integration, Software-Hardware Integration & Hardware-Hardware Integration. Thus, called as, System Integration Testing.

The greater the scope of integration, the more difficult it becomes to isolate defects to a specific component or system, which may lead to increased risk and additional time for troubleshooting.

It may be done in isolation from the rest of the system, depending on the context of the development life cycle and the system. Stubs, drivers and simulators may be used.

Understanding stub and driver in more detail

In the example above Component A calls Component B.

Now consider this, say I wanted to test that my Component A was functioning correctly but I had a dependency such that my component made calls to Component B and Component B was not yet ready.

What do I do? do I just wait for Component B to become ready? Well I could, or I can get creative and make a dummy Component B_Stub. Component B_Stub will act like Component B, it just will return whatever I want it to and thus I can continue my testing.

*In a situation like this, were I would create a **dummy component that my component to make calls to**, that dummy component is called a **STUB**.*

Now if I was the developer of Component B, and I was dependent on calls made from Component A. Say Component A was not ready as yet, and I wanted to test my Component B.

What do I do? do I just wait for Component A to become ready? Well I could, or I can get creative and make a dummy Component A_Driver. Component A_Driver will act like Component A. it just will simulate the calls I want it to and thus I can continue my testing.

*In this situation, were I would create a **dummy component that will make calls to my component**, that dummy component is called a **DRIVER**.*

Systematic integration strategies may be based on the:

- System architecture (such as top-down and bottom-up);
- Functional tasks;
- Transaction processing sequences.

In order to ease fault isolation and detect defects early, integration should normally be incremental rather than "big bang".

Testing of specific non-functional characteristics (e.g., performance) may be included in integration testing as well as functional testing.

At each stage of integration, testers concentrate solely on the integration itself.

For example, if they are integrating module A with module B they are interested in testing the communication between the modules, not the functionality of the individual module as that was done during component testing. Both functional and structural approaches may be used.

Ideally, testers should understand the architecture and influence integration planning. If integration tests are planned before components or systems are built, those components can be built in the order required for most efficient testing.

The **Test Basis** (Work product(s) being referenced for deriving test cases) for Integration Testing are:

- Software and system design
- Architecture
- Workflows
- Use cases

The typical **Test Objects** (i.e. what is being tested) for Integration Testing are:

- Sub-systems database implementation
- Infrastructure
- Interfaces
- System configuration and configuration data

The typical **Defects and Failures** for component integration testing include:

- Incorrect data, missing data, or incorrect data encoding
- Incorrect sequencing or timing of interface calls
- Interface mismatch
- Failures in communication between components
- Unhandled or improperly handled communication failures between components
- Incorrect assumptions about the meaning, units, or boundaries of the data being passed between components

Examples of typical **Defects and Failures** for system integration testing include:

- Inconsistent message structures between systems
- Incorrect data, missing data, or incorrect data encoding
- Interface mismatch
- Failures in communication between systems
- Unhandled or improperly handled communication failures between systems

2.2.4. System Testing

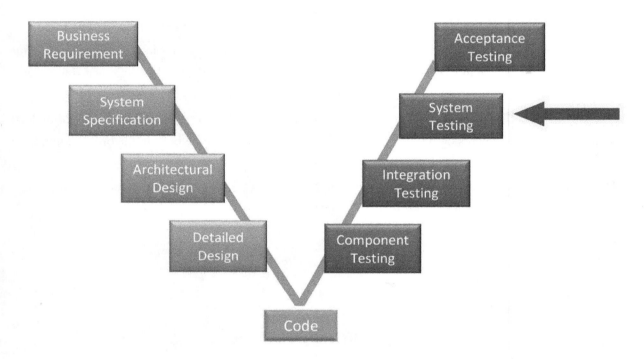

System testing is concerned with the behaviour of a whole system/product. The testing scope shall be clearly addressed in the Master and/or Level Test Plan for that test level.

Objectives of system testing include:

- Reducing risk
- Verifying whether the functional and non-functional behaviours of the system are as designed and specified
- Validating that the system is complete and will work as expected
- Building confidence in the quality of the system as a whole
- Finding defects
- Preventing defects from escaping to higher test levels or production

In system testing, the test environment should correspond to the final target or production environment as much as possible in order to minimize the risk of environment-specific failures not being found in testing.

System testing may include tests based on risks and/or on:

- Requirements specifications;
- Business processes;
- Use cases;
- Other high-level text descriptions or models of system behaviour;
- Interactions with the operating system; and
- System resources.

System testing should investigate functional and non-functional requirements of the system, and data quality characteristics.

Testers also need to deal with incomplete or undocumented requirements. System testing of functional requirements starts by using the most appropriate specification-based (black-box) techniques for the aspect of the system to be tested.

For example, a decision table may be created for combinations of effects described in business rules. Structure based techniques (white-box) may then be used to assess the thoroughness of the testing with respect to a structural element, such as menu structure or web page navigation.

An independent test team often carries out system testing.

The **Test Basis** (Work product(s) being referenced for deriving test cases) for System Testing are:

- System and software requirement specification
- Use cases
- Functional specification
- Risk analysis reports
- Models of system behaviour
- State diagrams
- System and user manuals

The typical **Test Objects** (i.e. what is being tested) for System Testing are:

- System, user and operation manuals
- System configuration and configuration data
- Hardware/software systems
- Operating systems

Examples of typical **Defects and Failures** for system testing include:

- Incorrect calculations
- Incorrect or unexpected system functional or non-functional behaviour
- Incorrect control and/or data flows within the system
- Failure to properly and completely carry out end-to-end functional tasks
- Failure of the system to work properly in the production environment(s)
- Failure of the system to work as described in system and user manuals

2.2.5. Acceptance Testing

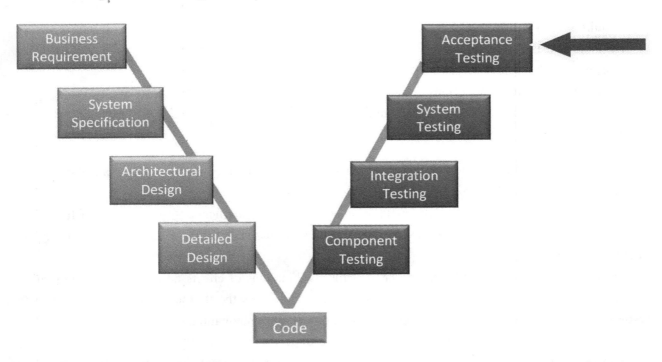

Acceptance testing is often the responsibility of the customers or users of a system; other stakeholders may be involved as well. If conducted by the customers or users its known as User acceptance testing whereas when tested internally with collaboration of customers, is known as Acceptance testing.

The goal in acceptance testing is to establish confidence in the system, parts of the system or specific non-functional characteristics of the system. Finding defects is not the main focus in acceptance testing.

Acceptance testing may assess the system's readiness for deployment and use, although it is not necessarily the final level of testing.

For example, a large-scale system integration test may come after the acceptance test for a system.

Acceptance testing may occur at various times in the life cycle, for example:

- A COTS software product may be acceptance tested when it is installed or integrated
- Acceptance testing of the usability of a component may be done during component testing
- Acceptance testing of a new functional enhancement may come before system testing

Organizations may use other terms as well, such as factory acceptance testing and site acceptance testing for systems that are tested before and after being moved to a customer's site.

Acceptance testing is conducted in two levels

- **Alpha Testing** – This level is performed by the customer or it's team before accepting the product and usually performed in the environment where it was developed and tested.
- **Beta Testing** – Once Alpha testing passes, customer accepts the software and deploys the system on real environment. Further, it is tested by the end users (real users) of the system/product. The objective of this level is extensive independent testing and collect feedback from real users.

Typical forms of acceptance testing include the following:

User Acceptance testing

- Typically verifies the fitness for use of the system by business users.

Operational (acceptance) testing

- The acceptance of the system by the system administrators, including:
- Testing of backup/restore
- Disaster recovery
- User management
- Maintenance tasks
- Data load and migration tasks
- Periodic checks of security vulnerabilities

Contract and regulation acceptance testing

- Contract acceptance testing is performed against a contract's acceptance criteria for producing custom-developed software.
- Acceptance criteria should be defined when the parties agree to the contract.
- Regulation acceptance testing is performed against any regulations that must be adhered to, such as government, legal or safety regulations.

Alpha and Beta (or field) testing

- Developers of market, or COTS, software often want to get feedback from potential or existing customers in their market before the software product is put up for sale commercially.
- Alpha testing is performed at the developing organization's site but not by the developing team.
- Beta testing, or field-testing, is performed by customers or potential customers at their own locations.

The **Test Basis** (Work product(s) being referenced for deriving test cases) for Acceptance Testing are:

- User requirements
- System requirements
- Use cases
- Business processes
- Risk analysis reports

The typical **Test Objects** (i.e. what is being tested) for Acceptance Testing are:

- Business processes on fully integrated system
- Operational and maintenance processes
- User procedures
- Forms

- Reports
- Configuration data

Examples of typical **Defects** for any form of acceptance testing include:

- System workflows do not meet business or user requirements
- Business rules are not implemented correctly
- System does not satisfy contractual or regulatory requirements
- Non-functional failures such as security vulnerabilities, inadequate performance efficiency under high loads, or improper operation on a supported platform

> Typically Asked: Test basis, Test Objects & Defects from each level.
> *#Tip: Use Cases are common test basis for integration, System & Acceptance testing whereas Risk Analysis report are common test basis for System & Acceptance Testing*

2.3. Test Types

2.3.1. Introduction

A group of test activities can be aimed at verifying the software system (or a part of a system) based on a specific reason or target for testing.

A test type is focused on a particular test objective, which could be any of the following:

- A function to be performed by the software
- A non-functional quality characteristic, such as reliability or usability
- The structure or architecture of the software or system
- Change related, i.e. confirming that defects have been fixed (confirmation testing) and looking for unintended changes (regression testing)

A model of the software may be developed and/or used in:

- Structural testing
  - o E.g. a control flow model or menu structure model

- Non-functional testing
  - o E.g. performance model, usability model, security threat modelling

- Functional testing
  - o E.g. a process flow model, a state transition model or a plain language specification

2.3.2. Functional Testing (Testing of Function)

The functions that a system, subsystem or component are to perform may be described in work products such as a requirements specification, use cases, or a functional specification, or they may be undocumented.

The functions are **"What"** the system does.

Functional tests are based on functions and features as described in documents or understood by the testers. It includes their interoperability with specific systems, and may be performed at all test levels.

E.g. Tests for components may be based on a component specification

Specification-based techniques may be used to derive test conditions and test cases from the functionality of the software or system. We will understand about techniques in more detail in chapter 4.

Functional testing considers the external behaviour of the software (black-box testing). The primary functional test levels are Unit Testing, Integration Testing, System Testing and Acceptance Testing. These levels generally determine the validation basic functionality without which, a feature or function cannot work.

All other levels, which you may know would be categorised under non-functional testing (NFT) and they deal with one or the other quality characteristics of the system/product.

There are certain non-functional features (test levels) which requires their core functional features to be determined and tested earlier during the functional levels and later elaborated for quality characteristics.

A type of functional testing, **security testing**, investigates the functions (e.g., a firewall) relating to detection of threats, such as viruses, from malicious outsiders.

Another type of functional testing, **interoperability testing**, evaluates the capability of the software product to interact with one or more specified components or systems.

2.3.3. Non-functional Testing (Software Quality Characteristics)

Non-functional testing includes, but is not limited to:

Performance testing
- The process of testing to determine the performance of a software product.
- See also efficiency testing.

Load testing
- A type of performance testing conducted to evaluate the behavior of a component or system with increasing load, e.g. numbers of parallel users and/or numbers of transactions, to determine what load can be handled by the component or system.

Stress testing

- A type of performance testing conducted to evaluate a system or component at or beyond the limits of its anticipated or specified work loads, or with reduced availability of resources such as access to memory or servers.

Usability testing

- Testing to determine the extent to which the software product is understood, easy to learn, easy to operate and attractive to the users under specified conditions.

Maintainability testing

- The process of testing to determine the maintainability of a software product.

Reliability testing

- The process of testing to determine the reliability of a software product

Portability testing / configuration testing

- The process of testing to determine the portability of a software product

It is the testing of **"How"** the system works.

Non-functional testing may be performed at all test levels. The term non-functional testing describes the tests required to measure characteristics of systems and software that can be quantified on a varying scale, such as response times for performance testing.

Non-functional testing considers the external behaviour of the software and in most cases uses black-box test design techniques to accomplish that and derive test conditions. Non-functional test design and execution may involve special skills or knowledge, such as knowledge of the inherent weaknesses of a design or technology (e.g., security vulnerabilities associated with particular programming languages) or the particular user base (e.g., the personas of users of healthcare facility management systems).

2.3.4. Testing of Software Structure/Architecture (Structural Testing)

Structural (white-box) testing may be performed at all test levels. Structural techniques are best used after specification-based techniques, in order to help measure the thoroughness of testing through assessment of coverage of a type of structure.

- **Coverage** is the extent that a structure has been exercised by a test suite, expressed as a percentage of the items being covered.
- If coverage is not 100%, then more tests may be designed to test those items that were missed to increase coverage.

Structural testing is conducted at all test levels, but especially in component testing and component integration testing levels, tools can be used to measure the code coverage of elements, such as statements or decisions.

WHITE BOX TESTING: Synonyms include – Structure Box Testing, Clear Box Testing, Open Box Testing, Transparent Box Testing, Glass Box Testing

Advantages of white-box testing include:

- Testing can be commenced at an earlier stage. One need not wait for the GUI to be available
- Testing is more thorough, with the possibility of covering most paths and achieve better coverage.

Disadvantages of white-box testing includes:

- Since tests can be very complex, highly skilled resources are required, with thorough knowledge of programming and implementation
- Test script maintenance can be a difficult if the implementation changes too frequently
- Since this method of testing it closely tied with the application being tested, tools to cater to every kind of implementation/platform may not be readily available.

2.3.5. Black Box Testing

Black Box Testing, also known as Behavioural Testing, is a software testing method in which the internal structure/design/implementation of the item being tested is not known to the tester. These tests can be functional or non-functional, though usually functional.

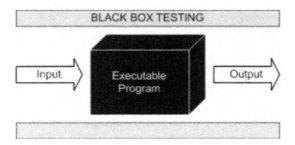

BLACK BOX TESTING: Synonyms include – Closed Box Testing, Skin Box Testing, Opaque Box Testing

This method is named so because the software program, from the understanding of the tester, is like a black box; inside which one cannot see.

Black Box Testing attempts to find defects in the following categories:

- Incorrect or missing functions
- Interface errors
- Errors in data structures or external database access

- Behaviour or performance errors
- Initialization and termination errors

Advantages of black box testing includes:

- Tests are done from a user's point of view and will help in exposing discrepancies in the specifications
- Tester need not know programming languages or how the software has been implemented
- Tests can be conducted by a body independent from the developers, allowing for an objective perspective and the avoidance of developer-bias
- Test cases can be designed as soon as the specifications are complete

Disadvantages of black box testing includes:

- Only a small number of possible inputs can be tested and many program paths will be left untested
- Without clear specifications, which is the situation in many projects, test cases will be difficult to design
- Tests can be redundant if the software designer/ developer has already run a test case
- Ever wondered why a soothsayer closes the eyes when foretelling events? So is almost the case in Black Box Testing.

Black Box testing is can be conducted at all test levels, but especially in system testing and acceptance testing levels, techniques are helpful to determine the coverage.

> There are no other color than white and black in software testing
> *#GREY BOX TESTING – It is type where a single person plays the role of developer as well as tester and uses a combined approach of white and black box testing. But due to contradiction with concept of Psychology of Testing, ISTQB® doesn't speak about it.*

2.3.6. Change Related Testing (Confirmation & Regression Testing)

After a defect is detected and fixed(resolved), the software should be re-tested to confirm that the original defect has been successfully removed. *This is called **Confirmation Testing** (Re-testing).* This is generally performed by re-executing the same test cases which revealed the defect.

It is also possible that due to the same defect there were many other test failures as well. In this instance, confirmation testing may involve re-execution of all these tests which were associated with the defect.

> #REMINDER - From chapter 1, we already know that Debugging (analysing and fixing a defect) is a development activity, not a testing activity.

Generally, to resolve an issue(defect) developer either adds new line of code, delete lines of code or modify existing lines of code. It is possible, these changes may invite some unwanted side-effects to the system. The defect reported may have been resolved, but it is equally important to check for any adverse side-effect, due to this fix. That's where, regression testing is performed which involves other test cases to be executed.

Regression testing may also be executed in few other scenarios where changes to an existing code is done. The instances where regressions are performed:

- When a defect is resolved
- When new piece of code is added to an existing application (Updates, Upgrades)
- When the system moves from one platform to another (Migration)

In all above cases, regression testing, will assure you that these changes have not introduced any defects in the system. Otherwise, it will help you detect those defects and get them resolved.

The extent of regression testing is based on the risk of not finding defects in software that was working previously. Tests should be repeatable if they are to be used for confirmation testing and to assist regression testing. Regression testing may be performed at all test levels, and includes functional, non-functional and structural testing.

Considering an application where the changes are frequent

An E-Commerce website having frequent changes in the product details, adding new products, etc
A Banking application being updated frequently for security, performance, usability, etc

Regression test suites are run many times. It's also important to keep adding new test cases with respect to updates to the existing test suite. **As regressions are executing quite often, regression testing is a strong candidate for automation.**

2.3.7. Test Types and Test Levels

It is possible to perform any of the test types mentioned above at any test level. To illustrate, examples of functional, non-functional, white-box, and change-related tests will be given across all test levels, for a banking application, starting with functional tests:

- For component testing, tests are designed based on how a component should calculate compound interest.
- For component integration testing, tests are designed based on how account information captured at the user interface is passed to the business logic.
- For system testing, tests are designed based on how account holders can apply for a line of credit on their checking accounts.
- For system integration testing, tests are designed based on how the system uses an external microservice to check an account holder's credit score.
- For acceptance testing, tests are designed based on how the banker handles approving or declining a credit application.

The following are examples of non-functional tests:

- For component testing, performance tests are designed to evaluate the number of CPU cycles required to perform a complex total interest calculation.

- For component integration testing, security tests are designed for buffer overflow vulnerabilities due to data passed from the user interface to the business logic.
- For system testing, portability tests are designed to check whether the presentation layer works on all supported browsers and mobile devices.
- For system integration testing, reliability tests are designed to evaluate system robustness if the credit score microservice fails to respond.
- For acceptance testing, usability tests are designed to evaluate the accessibility of the banker's credit processing interface for people with disabilities.

The following are examples of white-box tests:

- For component testing, tests are designed to achieve complete statement and decision coverage for all components that perform financial calculations.
- For component integration testing, tests are designed to exercise how each screen in the browser interface passes data to the next screen and to the business logic.
- For system testing, tests are designed to cover sequences of web pages that can occur during a credit line application.
- For system integration testing, tests are designed to exercise all possible inquiry types sent to the credit score microservice.
- For acceptance testing, tests are designed to cover all supported financial data file structures and value ranges for bank-to-bank transfers.

Finally, the following are examples for change-related tests:

- For component testing, automated regression tests are built for each component and included within the continuous integration framework.
- For component integration testing, tests are designed to confirm fixes to interface-related defects as the fixes are checked into the code repository.
- For system testing, all tests for a given workflow are re-executed if any screen on that workflow changes.
- For system integration testing, tests of the application interacting with the credit scoring microservice are re-executed daily as part of continuous deployment of that microservice.
- For acceptance testing, all previously-failed tests are re-executed after a defect found in acceptance testing is fixed.

2.4. Maintenance Testing

2.4.1. Introduction

Once deployed, a software system is often in service for years or decades. The maintenance of the system becomes crucial for organisation. During this time the system, its configuration data, or its environment are often corrected, changed or extended. Maintenance is also needed to preserve or improve non-functional quality characteristics of the component or system over its lifetime, especially performance efficiency, compatibility, reliability, security, compatibility, and portability.

> **MAINTENANCE TESTING:** Testing the changes to an operational system or the impact of a changed environment to an operational system. requirements.

The planning of releases in advance is crucial for successful maintenance testing. A distinction has to be made between planned releases and hot fixes. The scope of maintenance testing depends on:

- The degree of risk of the change, for example, the degree to which the changed area of software communicates with other components or systems
- The size of the existing system
- The size of the change

Maintenance testing is done on an existing operational system, and is triggered by modifications, migration, or retirement of the software or system.

2.4.2. Triggers for Maintenance

There are several reasons why software maintenance, and thus maintenance testing, takes place, both for planned and unplanned changes. The modifications which are triggers of maintenance can be classified as:

- Planned enhancement changes
  - Release-based
  - Corrective and emergency changes
  - Changes of environment
  - Planned upgrade of Commercial-Off-The-Shelf software
  - Patches to correct newly exposed or discovered vulnerabilities

- Migration related, such as
  - From one platform to another
  - Tests of data conversion

- Retirement, such as when an application reaches the end of its life

Maintenance testing for migration (e.g., from one platform to another) should include operational tests of the new environment as well as of the changed software. Migration testing (conversion testing) is also needed when data from another application will be migrated into the system being maintained.

Maintenance testing for the retirement of a system may include the testing of data migration or archiving if long data-retention periods are required.

For Internet of Things systems, maintenance testing may be triggered by the introduction of completely new or modified things, such as hardware devices and software services, into the overall system. The maintenance testing for such systems places particular emphasis on integration testing at different levels (e.g., network level, application level) and on security aspects, in particular those relating to personal data.

In addition to testing what has been changed, maintenance testing includes extensive regression testing to parts of the system that have not been changed.

> **The scope of maintenance testing is related to the risk of the change, the size of the existing system and to the size of the change.**

Depending on the changes, maintenance testing may be done at any or all test levels and for any or all test types.

2.4.3. Impact Analysis for Maintenance

Determining how the existing system may be affected by changes is called **Impact Analysis**, and is used to help decide how much regression testing to do and where. Impact analysis can also help to identify the areas in the system that will be affected by the change, identify the impact of a change on existing tests.

IMPACT ANALYSIS: The assessment of change to the layers of development documentation, test documentation and components, in order to implement a given change to specified requirements.

Impact analysis may be done before a change is made, to help decide if the change should be made, based on the potential consequences in other areas of the system. Impact analysis can be difficult if:

- Specifications (e.g., business requirements, user stories, architecture) are out of date or missing
- Test cases are not documented or are out of date
- Bi-directional traceability between tests and the test basis has not been maintained
- Tool support is weak or non-existent
- The people involved do not have domain and/or system knowledge
- Insufficient attention has been paid to the software's maintainability during development

> Maintenance testing can be difficult if specifications are out of date or missing, or testers with domain knowledge are not available.

Quick Revision & Tips on Chapter 2

1. Remember the difference in how testing is performed between different SDLC models.
2. It's very helpful to understand V-model to answer lot of questions related to this chapter.
3. Good characteristics of testing will have a question for sure.
4. The Test basis, Test objects & Typical defects will be critical area to expect question from this topic. Understand them, also the common test basis is key asset.
5. White and black box testing can be asked in different manner. In terms of definition, synonyms, difference, applied in levels, performed by, etc.
6. Understand the difference between confirmation testing & regression testing.
7. Applicability of regression testing and maintainability. Remember it is often automated.
8. Difference between functional and non-functional levels and where it can be performed.
9. In maintenance testing, triggers events, impact analysis and issues.
10. Topics like, Types of testing & Confirmation testing can include questions with multiple statements and you are asked with marking them true and false and finally pick the most relevant option.
11. Quite often the question in this chapter includes word like NOT or FALSE which means you need to pick the irrelevant option from given.
12. Quickly revise the bulleted point which would answer most of questions from this chapter.
13. This chapter will have 5 questions in the examination with following breakup.

Chapter 2 Question Distribution	K-Level	Number of Questions per LO	Suggested Points per question	
FL-2.1.2 FL-2.3.2	K1	Exactly ONE question based on either of these LOs is required.	1	**There is a total of 5 questions required for Chapter 2.** **K1 = 1** **K2 = 4** **K3 = 0** **Number of points for this chapter = 5**
FL-2.1.1 FL-2.2.1 FL-2.3.1 FL-2.3.3 FL-2.4.1 FL-2.4.2	K2	Exactly FOUR questions based on this set of 6 LOs are required. Each question must cover a DIFFERENT LO.	1	

 # For the exact topic number please refer the ISTQB® official syllabus.

Sample Questions on Chapter 2

1. **Repeated Testing of an already tested program, after modification, to discover any defects introduced or uncovered as a result of the changes in the software being tested or in another related or unrelated software component:**
   a) Re Testing
   b) Confirmation Testing
   c) Regression Testing
   d) Negative Testing

2. **Impact Analysis helps to decide**
   a) How much regression testing should be done.
   b) Exit Criteria
   c) How many more test cases need to written
   d) Different Tools to perform Regression Testing

3. **Non-functional system testing includes:**
   a) Testing to see where the system does not function properly
   b) Testing quality attributes of the system including performance and usability
   c) Testing a system feature using only the software required for that action
   d) Testing a system feature using only the software required for that function

4. **The difference between re-testing and regression testing is**
   a) Re-testing is running a test again; regression testing looks for unexpected side effects
   b) Re-testing looks for unexpected side effects; regression testing is repeating those tests
   c) Re-testing is done after faults are fixed; regression testing is done earlier
   d) Re-testing uses different environments, regression testing uses the same environment

5. **Which of the following is a characteristic of good testing and applies to any software development lifecycle model?**
   a) Acceptance testing is always the final test level to be applied
   b) All test levels are planned and completed for each developed feature
   c) Testers are involved as soon as the first piece of code can be executed
   d) For every development activity there is a corresponding testing activity.

6. **Alpha testing is:**
   a) post-release testing by end user representatives at the developer's site.
   b) the first testing that is performed.
   c) pre-release testing by end user representatives at the developer's site.
   d) pre-release testing by end user representatives at their sites.

7. **Testing activity which is performed to expose defects in the interfaces and in the interaction between integrated components is:**
    a) System Level Testing
    b) Integration Level Testing
    c) Unit Level Testing
    d) Component Testing

8. **Which of the following is an example of maintenance testing?**
    a) To test corrected defects during development of a new system.
    b) To test enhancements to an existing operational system.
    c) To handle complaints about system quality during user acceptance testing.
    d) To integrate functions during the development of a new system.

9. **Which of the following statements comparing component testing and system testing is TRUE?**
    a) Component testing verifies the functionality of software modules, program objects, and classes that are separately testable, whereas system testing verifies interfaces between components and interactions between different parts of the system.
    b) Test cases for component testing are usually derived from component specifications, design specifications, or data models, whereas test cases for system testing are usually derived from requirement specifications, functional specifications, or use cases.
    c) Component testing only focuses on functional characteristics, whereas system testing focuses on functional and non-functional characteristics.
    d) Component testing is the responsibility of the testers, whereas system testing typically is the responsibility of the users of the system.

10. **Which of the following statements about the benefits of deriving test cases from use cases are true and which are false?**
    A. **Deriving test cases from use cases is helpful for system and acceptance testing.**
    B. **Deriving test cases from use cases is helpful only for automated testing.**
    C. **Deriving test cases from use cases is helpful for component testing.**
    D. **Deriving test cases from use cases is helpful for integration testing.**
    a) A and D are true; B and C are false
    b) A is true; B, C, and D are false
    c) B and D are true; A and C are false
    d) A, C, and D are true; B is false

Answer to the questions can be found at the last page of the book

3. Static Testing

Terms: Ad hoc reviewing, Checklist-based reviewing, Dynamic testing, Formal review, Informal review, Inspection, Perspective-based reading, Review, Role-based reviewing, Scenario-based reviewing, Static analysis, Static testing, Technical review, Walkthrough

3.1. Static Techniques

3.1.1. Introduction

Let's re-cap quickly using the V-Model:

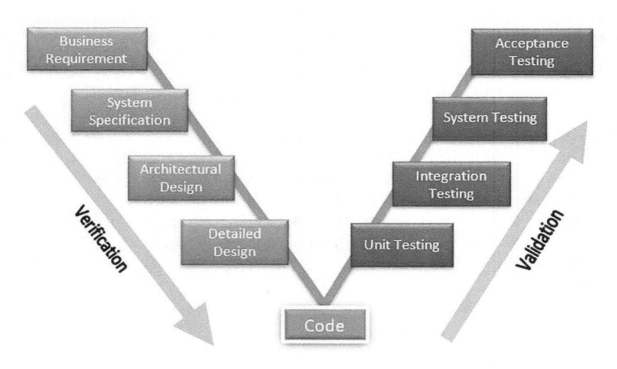

Static Testing is testing of a component or system at specification or implementation level without execution of that software.

When we test and we execute code during testing, we refer to that as: Dynamic Testing.

So, unlike dynamic testing, which requires the execution of software, static testing techniques rely on the manual examination (reviews) and automated or tool-based analysis (static analysis) of the code or other project documentation without the execution of the code.

3.1.2. Work Products that Can Be Examined by Static Testing

A review can be applied to any work product provided that the participants know how to read and understand codes. A review could be done entirely as a manual activity, but there is also tool support. The main manual activity is to examine a work product and make comments about it.

Any software work product can be reviewed, including:

- Requirements specifications (Function & Non-Functional)
- Epic, User stories & Acceptance criteria (In agile methodology)
- Design specifications
- Code
- Test plans, Test specifications and Test cases
- Test scripts
- User guides or manuals
- Web pages
- Contracts, Project Plans, Schedule and Budgets

3.1.3. Benefits of Static Testing

Reviews are a way of testing software work products (including code) and can be performed well before dynamic test execution. Defects detected during reviews early in the life cycle (e.g., defects found in requirements) are often much cheaper to remove than those detected by running tests on the executing code.

Think of it this way, if you were to pick up a defect in requirements generation, you have potentially saved all the time, and therefore cost of developers and testers developing and testing an incorrect specification and rework required to refactor performed activities.

The benefits of reviews include:

- Detecting and correcting defects more efficiently, and prior to dynamic test execution
- Identifying defects which are not easily found by dynamic testing (detailed elaboration in 3.1.4)
- Preventing defects in design or coding by uncovering inconsistencies, ambiguities, contradictions, omissions, inaccuracies, and redundancies in requirements
- Increasing development productivity (e.g., due to improved design, more maintainable code)
- Reducing development cost and time
- Reducing testing cost and time

- Reducing total cost of quality over the software's lifetime, due to fewer failures later in the lifecycle or after delivery into operation
- Improving communication between team members in the course of participating in reviews
- Review can find omissions. E.g., finding a missing requirement which may have been unlikely to find during dynamic testing.

3.1.4. Difference Between Static and Dynamic Testing

Reviews, static analysis and dynamic testing have the same objective – identifying defects. They are performed in different ways but complement each other by finding different defects. The different techniques can find different types of defects effectively and efficiently.

> Static techniques find causes of failures (defects) rather than the failures themselves.

Let's understand in more details how static is different from dynamic

Reviews and Static analysis are Static Testing Techniques.
Let's take a closer look at them

One main distinction is that static testing finds defects in work products directly rather than identifying failures caused by defects when the software is run. A defect can reside in a work product for a very long time without causing a failure. The path where the defect lies may be rarely exercised or hard to reach, so it will not be easy to construct and execute a dynamic test that encounters it. Static testing may be able to find the defect with much less effort.

Another distinction is that static testing can be used to improve the consistency and internal quality of work products, while dynamic testing typically focuses on externally visible behaviours.

Compared with dynamic testing, typical defects that are easier and cheaper to find and fix through static testing include:

- Requirement defects (e.g., inconsistencies, ambiguities, contradictions, omissions, inaccuracies, and redundancies)
- Design defects (e.g., inefficient algorithms or database structures, high coupling, low cohesion)
- Coding defects (e.g., variables with undefined values, variables that are declared but never used, unreachable code, duplicate code)
- Deviations from standards (e.g., lack of adherence to coding standards)
- Incorrect interface specifications (e.g., different units of measurement used by the calling system than by the called system)
- Security vulnerabilities (e.g., susceptibility to buffer overflows)
- Gaps or inaccuracies in test basis traceability or coverage (e.g., missing tests for an acceptance criterion)

3.2. Review Process

3.2.1. Introduction

The different types of reviews vary from informal to formal.

Informal reviews are characterized by:

- No written instructions for reviewers
- No formal process

Formal reviews are characterized by:

- Including team participation
- Documented results of the review and;
- Documented procedures for conducting the review

The formality of a review process is related to factors such as:

- The maturity of the development process
- Any legal or regulatory requirements
- The need for an audit trail

The way a review is carried out depends on the agreed objectives of the review. We may choose to perform reviews with a view to:

- Find defects
- Gain understanding
- Educate testers and new team members
- Discussion and decision by consensus

3.2.2. Work Product Review Process

The above diagram shows the main activities of a typical review process (also known as formal review process). Let's look at the sub-activities for each of the main activities.

During the **Planning**, Manager is responsible for most of the activity. The main activities include:

- Defining the scope of the review (which includes the purpose/objective of review)
- Identifying review characteristics (review types, roles, activities & checklist)
- Selecting the personnel

- Allocating roles
- Defining the entry and exit criteria for more formal review types (e.g., inspections)
- Selecting which parts of documents to review
- Checking entry criteria (for more formal review types)

During the **Initiate Review**, the moderator initiates the review by conducting following activities:

- Distributing the work product (physically or by electronic means) and other material, such as issue log forms, checklists, and related work products
- Explaining the scope, objectives, process, roles, and work products to the participants
- Answering any questions that participants may have about the review

During the **Individual Review (Individual Preparation)**, the main activities include:

- Reviewers start reviewing all or part of the work product, shared to them
- As they review, they make note of potential defects, recommendations, and questions

During the **Issue Communication and Analysis** (Review Meeting), all the defined roles will gather together to have joint discussion on the review findings. The main activities include:

- Communicating identified potential defects (e.g., in a review meeting)
- Analysing potential defects, assigning ownership and status to them
- Evaluating and documenting quality characteristics
- Evaluating the review findings against the exit criteria to make a review decision (reject; major changes needed; accept, possibly with minor changes)

During the **Fixing and Reporting** activity, the focus is on:

- Creating defect reports for those findings that require changes
- Fixing defects found (typically done by the author) in the work product reviewed
- Communicating defects to the appropriate person or team (when found in a work product related to the work product reviewed)
- Recording updated status of defects (in formal reviews), potentially including the agreement of the comment originator
- Gathering metrics (for more formal review types)
- Checking that exit criteria are met (for more formal review types)
- Accepting the work product when the exit criteria are reached

3.2.3. Roles and Responsibilities in A Formal Review

A formal review will include a Management (Manager), Facilitator (Moderator), Review Leader, Author, Reviewers and a Scribe (Recorder).

Author

- Creates the work product under review
- Fixes defects in the work product under review (if necessary)

Management

- Is responsible for review planning
- Decides on the execution of reviews
- Assigns staff, budget, and time
- Monitors ongoing cost-effectiveness
- Executes control decisions in the event of inadequate outcomes

Facilitator (often called moderator)

- Ensures effective running of review meetings (when held)
- Mediates, if necessary, between the various points of view
- Is often the person upon whom the success of the review depends

Review leader

- Takes overall responsibility for the review
- Decides who will be involved and organizes when and where it will take place

Reviewers

- May be subject matter experts, persons working on the project, stakeholders with an interest in the work product, and/or individuals with specific technical or business backgrounds
- Identify potential defects in the work product under review
- May represent different perspectives (e.g., tester, programmer, user, operator, business analyst, usability expert, etc.)

Scribe (or recorder)

- Collates potential defects found during the individual review activity
- Records new potential defects, open points, and decisions from the review meeting (when held)

Looking at software products or related work products from different perspectives and using checklists can make reviews more effective and efficient.

> *For example, a checklist based on various perspectives such as user, maintainer, tester or operations, or a checklist of typical requirements problems may help to uncover previously undetected issues.*

3.2.4. Types of Reviews

A single software product or related work product may be the subject of more than one review. If more than one type of review is used, the order may vary.

> *For example, an informal review may be carried out before a technical review, or an inspection may be carried out on a requirements specification before a walkthrough with customers.*

The main characteristics, options and purposes of common review types are:

Informal Review

Main purpose: inexpensive way to get some benefit, detecting defects ✺

- Possible additional purposes: generating new ideas or solutions, quickly solving minor problems
- **No formal process** ✺
- May not involve a review meeting
- May be performed by a colleague of the author (buddy check) or by more people
- Results may be documented
- Varies in usefulness depending on the reviewers
- Use of checklists is optional
- Very commonly used in Agile development

Walkthrough

Main purposes: find defects, improve the software product, consider alternative implementations, evaluate conformance to standards and specifications ✺

- Possible additional purposes: exchanging ideas about techniques or style variations, training of participants, achieving consensus
- Individual preparation before the review meeting is optional
- **Review meeting is typically led by the author of the work product** ✺
- Scribe is mandatory
- Use of checklists is optional
- May take the form of scenarios, dry runs, or simulations
- Potential defect logs and review reports may be produced · May vary in practice from quite informal to very formal

Technical Review

Main purposes: gaining consensus, detecting potential defects ✺

- Possible further purposes: evaluating quality and building confidence in the work product, generating new ideas, motivating and enabling authors to improve future work products, considering alternative implementations

All Power is within You!!

- **Reviewers should be technical peers of the author, and technical experts in the same or other disciplines ❀**
- Individual preparation before the review meeting is required
- Review meeting is optional, ideally led by a trained facilitator (typically not the author)
- Scribe is mandatory, ideally not the author
- Use of checklists is optional
- Potential defect logs and review reports are typically produced

> ❀ Points marked with this symbol are important to answer question from this chapter.

Inspection

Main purposes: detecting potential defects, evaluating quality and building confidence in the work product, preventing future similar defects through author learning and root cause analysis ❀

- Possible further purposes: motivating and enabling authors to improve future work products and the software development process, achieving consensus
- **Follows a defined process & formal documented outputs, based on rules and checklists ❀**
- Uses clearly defined roles, such as those which are mandatory, and may include a dedicated reader (who reads the work product aloud during the review meeting)
- Individual preparation before the review meeting is required
- Reviewers are either peers of the author or experts in other disciplines that are relevant to the work product
- **Specified entry and exit criteria are used ❀**
- Scribe is mandatory
- Review meeting is led by a trained facilitator (not the author)
- Author cannot act as the review leader, reader, or scribe
- Potential defect logs and review report are produced
- **Metrics are collected and used to improve the entire software development process, including the inspection process ❀**

> Walkthroughs, technical reviews and inspections can be performed within a peer group, i.e. colleagues at the same organizational level. This type of review is called a "peer review".

> #TIP: Activities in bold are unique points about each type of review which will help in examination

3.2.5. Applying Review Techniques

There are a number of review techniques that can be applied during the individual review (i.e., individual preparation) activity to uncover defects. These techniques can be used across the review types described above. The effectiveness of the techniques may differ depending on the type of review used. Examples of different individual review techniques for various review types are listed below.

Ad hoc

- In an ad hoc review, reviewers are provided with little or no guidance on how this task should be performed.
- Reviewers often read the work product sequentially, identifying and documenting issues as they encounter them.
- Ad hoc reviewing is a commonly used technique needing little preparation.
- This technique is highly dependent on reviewer skills and may lead to many duplicate issues being reported by different reviewers.

Checklist-based

- A checklist-based review is a systematic technique, whereby the reviewers detect issues based on checklists that are distributed at review initiation.
- A review checklist consists of a set of questions based on potential defects, which may be derived from experience.
- The main advantage of the checklist-based technique is a systematic coverage of typical defect types.
- Care should be taken not to simply follow the checklist in individual reviewing, but also to look for defects outside the checklist.

Scenario and Dry Runs

- In a scenario-based review, reviewers are provided with structured guidelines on how to read through the work product.
- A scenario-based approach supports reviewers in performing "dry runs" on the work product based on expected usage of the work product (if the work product is documented in a suitable format such as use cases).

Role Based

- A role-based review is a technique in which the reviewers evaluate the work product from the perspective of individual stakeholder roles.
- Typical roles include specific end user types (experienced, inexperienced, senior, child, etc.), and specific roles in the organization (user administrator, system administrator, performance tester, etc.).

Perspective Based

- In perspective-based reading, similar to a role-based review, reviewers take on different stakeholder viewpoints in individual reviewing. Typical stakeholder viewpoints include end user, marketing, designer, tester, or operations.
- In addition, perspective-based reading also requires the reviewers to attempt to use the work product under review to generate the product they would derive from it.
- Empirical studies have shown perspective-based reading to be the most effective general technique for reviewing requirements and technical work products.

3.2.6. Success Factors for Reviews

In order to have a successful review, the appropriate type of review and the techniques must be considered. In addition, there are a number of other factors that will affect the outcome of the review. The success factors aren't just one person's responsibility. Everyone must contribute efficiently specific to their responsibility to make a review successful.

Broadly, the success factors can be classified or separated in two categories – Organisational factors and People factor. Where, organisation relates to management and people relates to different roles within different types of review.

Organizational success factors for reviews include:

- Each review has clear objectives, defined during review planning, and used as measurable exit criteria
- Review types are applied which are suitable to achieve the objectives and are appropriate to the type and level of software work products and participants
- Any review techniques used, such as checklist-based or role-based reviewing, are suitable for effective defect identification in the work product to be reviewed
- Any checklists used address the main risks and are up to date
- Large documents are written and reviewed in small chunks, so that quality control is exercised by providing authors early and frequent feedback on defects
- Participants have adequate time to prepare
- Reviews are scheduled with adequate notice
- Management supports the review process (e.g., by incorporating adequate time for review activities in project schedules)

People-related success factors for reviews include:

- The right people are involved to meet the review objectives, for example, people with different skill sets or perspectives, who may use the document as a work input
- Testers are seen as valued reviewers who contribute to the review and learn about the work product, which enables them to prepare more effective tests, and to prepare those tests earlier
- Participants dedicate adequate time and attention to detail
- Reviews are conducted on small chunks, so that reviewers do not lose concentration during individual review and/or the review meeting (when held)
- Defects found are acknowledged, appreciated, and handled objectively
- The meeting is well-managed, so that participants consider it a valuable use of their time
- The review is conducted in an atmosphere of trust; the outcome will not be used for the evaluation of the participants
- Participants avoid body language and behaviours that might indicate boredom, exasperation, or hostility to other participants
- Adequate training is provided, especially for more formal review types such as inspections
- A culture of learning and process improvement is promoted

Quick Revision & Tips on Chapter 3

1. Remember the difference static and dynamic testing.
2. Static Testing and Static Analysis & Dynamic Testing and Dynamic Analysis are different.
3. Typical defects which can be identified by static testing are important.
4. Remember the activities of a formal review including the name of the main stages in right sequence.
5. The formal review's, roles in formal review and types of review are commonly asked as match the following.
6. This can be assisted by uniquely understanding the activities of each review.
7. Understand the different types of review and be able to differentiate between them.
8. Review techniques are simple and easy to remember. You can except a direct question.
9. Factors can be specific to organisation or people or some time you can be asked a common question about factors.
10. It's possible that you can expect one question using NOT or FALSE which means you need to pick the irrelevant option from given.
11. Quickly revise the bulleted point which would answer most of questions from this chapter.
12. This chapter will have 5 questions in the examination with following breakup.

Chapter 3 Question Distribution	K-Level	Number of Questions per LO	Suggested Points per question	
FL-3.1.1 FL-3.2.2	K1	Exactly ONE question based on either of these LOs is required.	1	**There is a total of 5 questions required for Chapter 3.** **K1 = 1**
FL-3.1.2 FL-3.1.3 FL-3.2.1 FL-3.2.3	K2	Exactly THREE questions based on this set of 5 LOs are required.	1	**K2 = 3** **K3 = 1**
FL-3.2.5		Each question must cover a DIFFERENT LO.		**Number of points for this chapter = 5**
FL-3.2.4	K3	Exactly ONE question based on this LO is required.	1	

 # For the exact topic number please refer the ISTQB® official syllabus.

Sample Question on Chapter 3

1. **The Initiate Review phase of a formal review includes the following:**
   a) Explaining the objective
   b) Fixing defects found typically done by author
   c) Follow up
   d) Individual Meeting preparations

2. **What is the main difference between a walkthrough and an inspection?**
   a) An inspection is lead by the author, whilst a walkthrough is lead by a trained moderator
   b) An inspection has a trained leader, whilst a walkthrough has no leader
   c) Authors are not present during inspections, whilst they are during walkthroughs
   d) A walkthrough is lead by the author, whilst an inspection is lead by a trained moderator

3. **Which of the following will NOT be detected by static analysis?**
   a) Parameter type mismatches
   b) Errors in requirements
   c) Undeclared variables
   d) Uncalled functions

4. **Which of the review types below is the BEST option to choose for reviewing safety critical components in a software project?**
   a) Informal Review
   b) Peer Review
   c) Inspection
   d) Walkthrough

5. **Which of the following statements about tool-supported static analysis is FALSE?**
   a) Tool-supported static analysis can be used as a preventive measure with appropriate processes in place.
   b) Tool-supported static analysis can find defects that are not easily found by dynamic testing.
   c) Tool-supported static analysis can result in cost savings by finding defects early.
   d) Tool-supported static analysis is a good way to force failures into the software.

6. **Which of the following describes the main phases of a formal review?**
   a) Initiation, status, individual preparation, review meeting, rework, follow up
   b) Planning, initiate review, individual review, issue communication and analysis, fixing and reporting
   c) Planning, kick off, individual review, fixing and reporting
   d) Individual preparation, review meeting, rework, closure, follow up, root cause analysis

7. **Who is responsible for documenting all the issues, problems and open point that were identified during the review meeting?**
   a) Moderator
   b) Scribe
   c) Reviewers
   d) Author

8. **What is the main purpose of Informal review?**
   a) Inexpensive way to get some benefit
   b) Find defects
   c) Learning, gaining understanding, effect finding
   d) Discuss, make decisions, solve technical problems

9. **Which of the following statements regarding static testing is FALSE:**
   a) Static testing requires the running of tests through the code
   b) Static testing finds defect which can not be easily found by dynamic testing
   c) Static testing includes techniques such as reviews and inspections
   d) Static testing can give measurements such as cyclomatic complexity

10. **Which of the following CORRECTLY matches the roles and responsibilities in a formal review?**
    a) Manager – Decides on the execution of reviews
    b) Review Leader - Ensures effective running of review meetings
    c) Scribe – Fixes defects in the work product under review
    d) Moderator – Monitors ongoing cost-effectiveness

Answer to the questions can be found at the last page of the book

Chapter 4

Test Techniques

4. Test Techniques

Terms: Black-box test technique, Boundary value analysis, Checklist-based testing, Coverage, Decision coverage, Decision table testing, Error guessing, Equivalence partitioning, Experience-based test technique, Exploratory testing, State transition testing, Statement coverage, Test technique, Use case testing, White-box test technique.

4.1. Introduction

The test development process described in this section can be done in different ways, from very informal with little or no documentation, to very formal.

The level of formality depends on:

- the context of the testing,
- the maturity of testing and development processes,
- time constraints,
- safety or regulatory requirements, and
- the people involved

During test analysis, the test basis documentation is analysed in order to determine what to test, i.e. to identify the test conditions.

A test condition is defined as an item or event that could be verified by one or more test cases

e.g., a function, transaction, quality characteristic or structural element

TRACEABILITY: The ability to identify related items in documentation and software, such as requirements with associated tests.

Establishing traceability from test conditions back to the specifications and requirements enables both effective impact analysis when requirements change, and determining requirements coverage for a set of tests.

During test analysis the detailed test approach is implemented to select the test design techniques to use based on, among other considerations, the identified.

TEST TECHNIQUES: These techniques are helpful in minimizing the test cases with maximum coverage. As exhaustive testing is impossible.

During test design the test cases and test data are created and specified.

A test case consists of:

- a set of input values
- execution preconditions
- expected results and
- execution post conditions

developed to cover a certain test objective(s) or test condition(s).

TEST DESIGN SPECIFICATION: A document specifying the test conditions (coverage items) for a test item, the detailed test approach and identifying the associated high level test cases.

TEST CASE SPECIFICATION: A document specifying a set of test cases (objective, inputs, test actions, expected results, and execution preconditions) for a test item.

Expected results should be produced as part of the specification of a test case and include outputs, changes to data and states, and any other consequences of the test. If expected results have not been defined, then a plausible, but erroneous, result may be interpreted as the correct one. Expected results should ideally be defined prior to test execution.

TEST PROCEDURE SPECIFICATION: A document specifying a sequence of actions for the execution of a test. Also known as test script or manual test script.

During test implementation the test cases are developed, implemented, prioritized and organized in the test procedure specification. The test procedure specifies the sequence of actions for the execution of a test. If tests are run using a test execution tool, the sequence of actions is specified in a test script (which is an automated test procedure).

The various test procedures and automated test scripts are subsequently formed into a test execution schedule that defines the order in which the various test procedures, and possibly automated test scripts, are executed. The test execution schedule will take into account such factors as regression tests, prioritization, and technical and logical dependencies.

4.2. Categories of Test Techniques

4.2.1. Choosing Test Techniques

Selecting a test technique depends on a number of factors, which includes:

- Type of component or system, component or system complexity
- Regulatory standards
- Customer or contractual requirements
- Risk levels, Risk types
- Test objectives
- Available documentation
- Tester knowledge and skills
- Software development lifecycle model
- Previous experience with using the test techniques on the component or system to be tested
- The types of defects expected in the component or system

Some techniques are more applicable to certain situations and test levels; others are applicable to all test levels. When creating test cases, testers generally use a combination of test techniques to achieve the best results from the test effort.

4.2.2. Categories of Test Techniques and their Characteristics

The purpose of a test design technique is to identify test conditions, test cases, and test data.

Test techniques covered in the foundation level syllabus are classified as being either black-box or white-box.

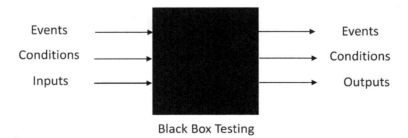

Black-box test design techniques (also called **behavioural, behaviour-based or specification-based techniques**) are a way to derive and select test conditions, test cases, or test data based on an analysis of the test basis documentation. This includes both functional and non-functional testing. Black-box testing, by definition, does not use any information regarding the internal structure of the component or system to be tested.

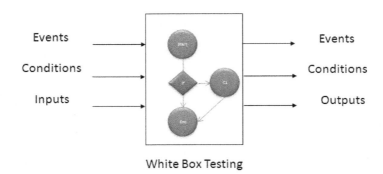

White Box Testing

White-box test design techniques (also called **structural or structure-based techniques**) are based on an analysis of the structure of the component or system.

Black-box and white-box testing may also draw upon the experience of developers, testers and users to determine what should be tested.

This syllabus refers to behaviour-based test design techniques as black-box techniques and structure-based test design techniques as white-box techniques.

The following techniques will be covered as a part of this syllabus:

Common characteristics of behaviour-based test design techniques include:

- Models, either formal or informal, are used for the specification of the problem to be solved, the software or its components
- Test cases can be derived systematically from these models

Common characteristics of structure-based test design techniques include:

- Information about how the software is constructed is used to derive the test cases (e.g., code and detailed design information)
- The extent of coverage of the software can be measured for existing test cases, and further test cases can be derived systematically to increase coverage

Common characteristics of experience-based test design techniques include:

- The knowledge and experience of people are used to derive the test cases
- The knowledge of testers, developers, users and other stakeholders about the software, its usage and its environment is one source of information
- Knowledge about typical defects and their distribution is another source of information

- Black Box Techniques
  - o Equivalence Partitioning
  - o Boundary Value Analysis
  - o Decision Table Testing
  - o State Transition Testing
  - o Use Case Testing

- White Box Techniques
  - o Statement Testing or Coverage
  - o Decision Testing or Coverage

- Experience Based Techniques
  - o Error Guessing
  - o Exploratory Testing
  - o Checklist Based Testing

> #TIP: This classification is important as this can be asked as question in the exam that which technique falls under which category.

4.3. Black Box Test Techniques

4.3.1. Equivalence Partitioning (EP)

In equivalence partitioning, inputs to the software or system are divided into groups/ranges/ classes that are expected to behave same, so they are likely to give the same output. Equivalence partitions are groups of values, if used will result in the system processing it in the same way.

Eg. Consider the following example:

> **"The system must approve the credit request if the amount requested is greater than $50 and less than $100"**

Let's represent this on a line:

1. First, we draw a line and represent the key values (Valid Range); in this case it's the range in between $51 and $99 as it says greater than $50 and less than $100, that the system will accept.

$51 to $99

2. Now let's add the second range which includes anything equals to or greater than $100 and this will be considered as Invalid, as this is out of valid range.

	$51 to $99	$100 ≤

3. Next, include the left side range as there is possibility that the value can be less than or equal to $50. But, in these cases, its very important to remember that the left side's least value will be $0 as payable value can't be negative. If it's negative it's not payable. Either way it means that the least value for the first range will be considered as zero.

≤ $50	$51 to $99	$100 ≤

4. At last we conclude that, there are three ranges or equivalence classes. Where, 1 is valid and other 2 are invalid ranges as shown in the table below. And minimum number of test cases required to cover this scenario is 3. As we take 1 test from each partition.

Invalid	Valid	Invalid
≤ $50	$51 to $99	$100 ≤
●	●	●

We now have 3 ranges,

1. Amounts between $51 and $99 are accepted
2. Amounts greater than $99 are rejected
3. Amounts less than $51 rand are rejected

Equivalence partitions (or classes) can be found for both valid data, i.e. values that should be accepted and invalid data, i.e. values that should be rejected.

Partitions can also be identified for:

- Outputs
- Internal values
- Time-related values (e.g., before or after an event)
- Interface parameters (e.g., integrated components being tested during integration testing)

Tests can be designed to cover all valid and invalid partitions.

Equivalence partitioning is applicable at all levels of testing. What this means is that you can use this test design technique to derive unit test, integration tests, system tests and even user acceptance tests.

> # SUMMARY ✿
> \# EP divides a given scenario into equivalence partitions/classes/ranges.
> \# All the elements/value of the same partitions are expected to behave same.
> \# Thus, as per EP we take only 1 test from each partition.
> \# EP is helpful to derive test cases at all level and for valid as well invalid.
> \# To achieve 100% coverage on a scenario we must cover all partitions in the scenario.
> \# Specifications are basis for applying equivalence partition.

Equivalence Partitioning – Sample Exam Question

In a system designed to work out the tax to be paid:
An employee has $ 4000 of salary tax free. The next $ 1500 is taxed at 10%. The next $ 28000 is taxed at 22%. Any further amount is taxed at 40%.

Which of these groups of numbers would fall into the same equivalence class?

a) $4800; $14000; $28000
b) $5200; $5500; $28000
c) $28001; $32000; $35000
d) $5800; $28000; $32000

When solving questions like this, I would like to get an understanding of what the scenario is, so that I can represent it in terms of a line. So from the above here is what I gather:

1. An employee has $4000 of salary tax free.
    a. This means that the initial $4000 of salary is tax free. Hence, we can say: If Amount of Salary is greater than or equal to $ 0 and less than or equal to $ 4000 then
        TAX = 0% (Amount of Salary)
        Note: Salary can't be negative so least possible input is $0

2. The next $1500 (next means above $4000) is taxed at 10%.
    a. This means the salary above $4000 and less than or equal to $5500 is taxed at 10%. So, for Salary between $4001 and $5500,
        TAX = 10% (Amount of Salary)

3. The next $28000 (means $28000 above $5500) is taxed at 22%.
    a. This means that if the salary greater than $5500, and less than or equal to $33500 is taxed at 22%. So, for salary between $5501 and $33500,
        TAX = 22% (Amount of Salary)

4. Any further amount is taxed at 40%

    a. This means that if the salary greater $33500, is taxed at 40%. So, for salary above $33500

       TAX = 40%

Here's the information represented on line:

EC1: 0% TAX	EC2: 10% TAX	EC3: 22% TAX	EC 4: 40% TAX
0-4000	4001-5500	5501-33500	33500 <

So we have 4 distinct areas. Let's look at each of the answers and see which option is right.

Answer	Number 1 (EC)	Number 2 (EC)	Number 3 (EC)	Same Equivalence Class?
A	$4800 (EC = 2)	$14000 (EC = 3)	$28000 (EC = 3)	No, EC 2 and EC 3
B	$5200 (EC = 2)	$5500 (EC = 2)	$28000 (EC = 3)	No, EC 2 and EC 3
C	$28001 (EC = 3)	$32000 (EC = 3)	$35000 (EC = 4)	No, EC 3 and EC 4
D	$5800 (EC = 3)	$28000 (EC = 3)	$32000 (EC = 3)	YES

So, the correct answer to this question is D

> #TIP: In EP, the right answer depends on your carefulness about reading the operators. Like "greater than" & "greater than or equals to" will have different values in range.
>
> Between, mathematically means inclusive of both the values. E.g, "Between 25 and 40" means the range is 25 to 40 not 26 to 39.

4.3.2. Boundary Value Analysis (BVA)

Boundary value analysis is an expansion of equivalence partioning. As per EP, we take one test from each partition. When we started testing using this technique, we realised that the behaviour at the edge(boundary) of each equivalence partition is more likely to be incorrect than behaviour within the partition. It is possible for humans to do mistake while defining the boundary values of a range, so boundaries are an area where testing is likely to yield defects.

The maximum and minimum values of a partition are its boundary values. Or say it as lower and upper boundary of a range.

- A boundary value for a valid partition is a valid boundary value;
- A boundary of an invalid partition is an invalid boundary value.

Tests can be designed to cover both valid and invalid boundary values. When designing test cases, a test for each boundary value is chosen. Boundary value analysis can be applied at all test levels. It is relatively easy to apply and its defect-finding capability is high. Detailed specifications are helpful in determining the interesting boundaries. This technique is often considered as an extension of equivalence partitioning or other black-box test design techniques. It can be used on equivalence classes for user input on screen as well as, for example, on time ranges (e.g., time out, transactional speed requirements) or table ranges (e.g., table size is 256*256).

Let's us understand using the same example which will be easy to follow:

The system must approve the credit request if the amount requested is greater than $50 and less than $100

We identified the following partitions:

≤ $50	$51 to $99	$100 ≤

The valid and invalid ranges are identified in the similar way. The boundary values will be measured on both side of each boundary (represented by dots in diagram below):

The boundary values can also be calculated as LB, LB-1, RB, RB+1. Where, LB (Left Boundary) and RB (Right Boundary) are the boundary values of valid range. So, here the boundary values are 50, 51, 99, 100. Here, 51 & 99(LB & RB) are valid and 50 & 100 (LB-1 & RB+1) are invalid.

SUMMARY ✿
\# BVA is stronger technique than EP.
\# BVA tests strictly on the boundaries of a given range.
\# There are two ways to apply BVA – Two-Point Analysis & Three-Point Analysis.
\# For 2-point analysis boundary values are calculated as LB, LB-1, RB, RB+1.
\# For 3-point analysis boundary values are calculated as LB, LB-1,LB+1, RB, RB+1, RB-1.
\# Specifications are basis for applying boundary value analysis.

Boundary Value Analysis – Sample Exam Question

A text field in an application accepts age of the user as input, in whole numbers. Here, the values allowed to be accepted by the field is between 18 to 30 years, inclusive of both the values. By

applying Boundary value analysis what is the minimum number of test cases required for maximum coverage?

a) 2

b) 3

c) 1

d) 4

Let's look at what our boundaries are:

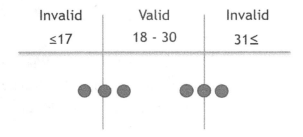

So, the possible boundary values are: 17, 18, 30, 31 and the right answer is D.

> **NOTE:** This approach of BVA is called as two-point boundary value analysis. Let's, see the same example with three-point boundary value analysis.

Let's look at the boundary values as per three-point analysis

As per three-point analysis the boundary values are considered as

LB, LB-1, LB+1 & RB, RB-1, RB+1 and the values are 17, 18, 19 & 29, 30, 31.

In this case, we take 3 values on each boundary (on the boundary, inside the boundary and outside the boundary). Thus, we will get 6 Boundary values where, 4 are valid (LB, LB+1, RB, RB-1) and 2 invalids (LB-1, RB+1).

4.3.3. Decision Table Testing (DTT)

Decision tables are a good way to capture system requirements that contain logical conditions, and to document internal system design. They may be used to record complex business rules that a system is to implement.

When creating decision tables, the specification is analysed, and conditions and actions of the system are identified. On a decision table, we first state all conditions then all actions:

Input Conditions	Condition 1
	Condition 2
Actions	Action 1
	Action 2
	Action 3

The input conditions and actions are most often stated in such a way that they must be true or false (Boolean).

For situations where the input is either true or false, the total number of possible combinations is calculated by raising 2 to the power of the number of conditions. The 2 represents the two options, true or false.

In the example above we have 2 conditions. The total number of possible combinations is thus $2^2 = 4$. This gives us a total of 4 combinations of True or False. Each combination is called as a test case. We represent each combination as a column on the table as follows:

		Combination/Test Cases			
		1	2	3	4
Input Conditions	Condition 1				
	Condition 2				
Actions	Action 1				
	Action 2				
	Action 3				

Each column of the table corresponds to a business rule that defines a unique combination of conditions and which result in the execution of the actions associated with that rule. The coverage standard commonly used with decision table testing is to have at least one test per column in the table, which typically involves covering all combinations of triggering conditions.

The strength of decision table testing is that it creates combinations of conditions that otherwise might not have been exercised during testing. It may be applied to all situations when the action of the software depends on several logical decisions.

In the case of Boolean inputs, we plot each combination as either using True/False or Yes/No as shown below:

		Combination Number			
		1	2	3	4
Input Conditions	Condition 1	Y	Y	N	N
	Condition 2	Y	N	Y	N
Actions	Action 1				
	Action 2				
	Action 3				

Remember, each column of the table corresponds to a business rule that defines a unique combination of conditions and which result in the execution of the actions associated with that rule. Hence, we plot the actions based on what the test basis defines as the expected result for the given set of inputs.

This is relatively simple when the number of choices for each condition is 2 (Y and N or True and False). When the number of choices for each condition varies it can get a bit complex, but this type of examples is not in scope of foundation level (this is discussed in advance level test analyst) so, let's not confuse ourselves. Rather. Let's look at an example of 3 condition inputs where, the test cases will be 2^3 and the count of test cases will be 8:

		Combination/Test Case							
		1	2	3	4	5	6	7	8
Input Conditions	Condition 1	Y	Y	Y	N	N	N	N	Y
	Condition 2	Y	Y	N	N	N	Y	Y	N
	Condition 3	Y	N	N	N	Y	Y	N	Y
Actions	Action 1								

SUMMARY ✿
DTT is used for scenarios where multiple conditions define specific output.
These outputs/actions are determined by various combination of given conditions.
Each combination is called as a test case.
Different scenario can have different count of conditions and measured as 2^n
Specifications are basis for applying Decision Table Testing.

Decision Table Testing – Sample Exam Question

#TIP: In foundation level exam, the questions on DTT will consist of the table. You don't have to worry about creating the table. All you have to do is understand the given table, follow the scenario asked and answer correct. Like the example below.

What is the expected result for each of the following test cases?

	Rule 1	Rule 2	Rule 3	Rule 4
Conditions				
Citibank Card Member	Yes	Yes	No	No
Type of Room	Silver	Platinum	Silver	Platinum
Actions				
Offer upgrade to Gold Luxury	Yes	No	No	No
Offer upgrade to Silver	N/A	Yes	N/A	No

X. Citibank card member, holding a Silver room?

Y. Non-Citibank member, holding a Platinum room?

a) X – Don't offer any upgrade, Y – Don't offer any upgrade.

b) X – Don't offer any upgrade, Y – Offer upgrade to Gold.

c) X – Offer upgrade to Silver, Y – Offer upgrade to Silver.

d) X – Offer upgrade to Gold, Y – Don't offer any upgrade.

In this example, first we have to understand the given table for different conditions, the combinations and their respective outcomes/actions.

In the given table, Condition 1 is Citibank Card Member – Y/N and Condition 2 is Type of Room – Silver/Platinum. There are actions provided to you in table for different combinations. Now, lets take the asked scenario and answer:

X. Citibank Card Member, holding a Silver Room?

The given scenario is covered in Rule 1 and the corresponding action for it is Offer upgrade to Gold Luxury.

Y. Non-Citibank member, holding a Platinum room?

The given scenario is covered in Rule 4 and the corresponding action for it is No, which means don not offer any upgrade to the customer.

Thus, the right answer is D

4.3.4. State Transition Testing (STT)

State transition testing is ideal when testing sequences of events that occur and were, we would want to verify correct handling of an event and particular conditions that applies to that event.

Tests can be designed:

- to cover a typical sequence of states
- to cover every state
- to exercise every transition
- to exercise specific sequences of transitions
- to test invalid transitions

State transition testing is much used within the embedded software industry and technical automation in general. However, the technique is also suitable for modelling a business object having specific states or testing screen-dialogue flows (e.g., for Internet applications or business scenarios).

Sample Example of a state based item:

The Electric Kettle

The various states that the kettle will be in at any single point of time is:

- Empty
- Full
- Turned On
- Turned Off
- Hot
- Cold etc

As you can see, the kettle will exhibit a different response depending on current conditions or previous history of its current state.

In the same way a system may exhibit a different response depending on current conditions or previous history of its current state. A system state defines the current condition of a system at a given time.

In a given state, the system will:

- Process only certain inputs
- Permit the system state to change to certain other states

Designers will use state diagrams to document the valid states that a system can take.

#TIP: A State Transition diagram is used to apply state transition testing technique, where state transition diagram is pictorial representation of a scenario which shows different STATES and various possible TRANSITIONS between them.

State Transition Diagrams

The following is a simple State transition diagram:

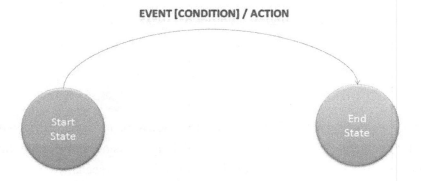

Let me explain how this diagram is exhibited. A state transition diagram consists of:

1. One or more **states** that the system or software can be in; this is represented by a circle. States are usually labelled to describe that state of the system to the reader. For example an ATM might have an initial state of idle, dispensing cash or awaiting pin

2. One or more **transitions**; this is represented by an arrow. The transition represents the change of the systems current state to its new state. In order to be clear to the reader, the designer will document the **event** that will trigger the change in the systems state, the **condition** under which that condition is executed and the **action** of the system as it changes (or transitions) from its current state to its new state.

This might be a lot to take in, but it is very simple. Consider a Gumball Machine. It's normally in idle state. Then a little kid walks up and inserts a $1 coin, turns the switch, and look at that out pops a gumball. What genius! Now, let's look at all the states that this simple contraption can be in.

To begin with it, let's consider its initial idle state;

The event of the switch being turned under the condition that a valid coin has being inserted changes the state of the machine from idle to dispensing gumball and then immediately back to idle

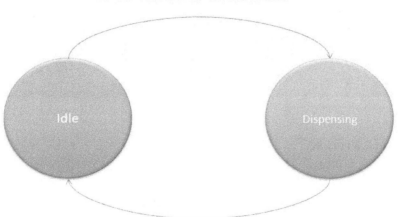

But what happens if the coin is invalid, for whatever reason. Surely, we must be clear about how the system should behave. In the event that the switch is turned and the coin is invalid, the system should return the coin and remain in its initial idle state.

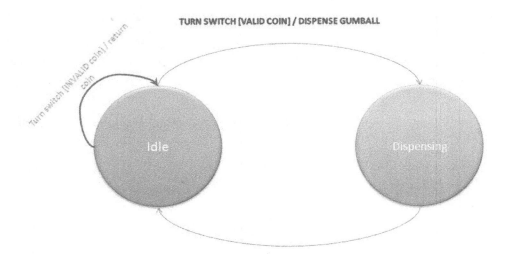

TURN SWITCH [VALID COIN] / DISPENSE GUMBALL

The example above is a simple one, but it should give you a better understanding of how the states of a system can be represented by such a diagram.

To a tester, a state transition diagram allows him/her to view the software in terms of its states, transitions between states, the inputs or events that trigger state changes (transitions) and the actions which may result from those transitions. The focus is whether the system changes states correctly.

> The states of the system or object under test are:
>
> - Separate
> - Identifiable and
> - Finite in number

State Transitions and Coverage

In some cases, the sequences of events can be infinite. Testing however cannot go on indefinitely because we work in a world where we are constrained by time and money to name but a few. How do we know that we have done enough testing?

We can define the level of coverage we want to achieve based on risk.

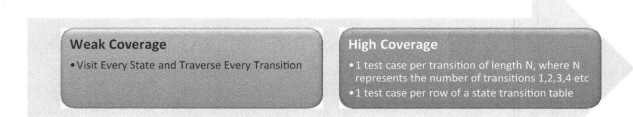

Weak Coverage
- Visit Every State and Traverse Every Transition

High Coverage
- 1 test case per transition of length N, where N represents the number of transitions 1,2,3,4 etc
- 1 test case per row of a state transition table

All Power is within You!!

Chow's Switch Coverage

Professor Chow developed the coverage called Chows Switch Coverage. It is also known as N-1 switch coverage.

So, if you wanted to cover all transitions of:

- Length 1, then N = 1 and N-1 = 0 so you get 0-switch coverage.
- Length 2, then N = 2 and N-1 = 1 so you get 1-switch coverage.
- Length 3, then N = 3 and N-1 = 2 so you get 2-switch coverage.
- Length 4, then N = 4 and N-1 = 3 so you get 3-switch coverage.

Etc . . .

The Chow's principle is to address that there is a possibility of driving various test cases using state transition but, this is not in scope of Foundation level syllabus. So, let's keep this book to the point and crisp with respect to examination.

Sample Exam Question:

Given the following state model of a battery charger software:

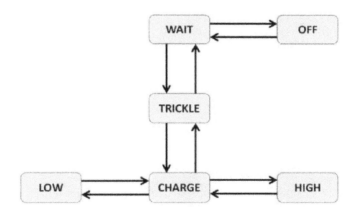

Which of the following sequences of transitions provides the highest level of transition coverage for the model?

a.   OFF → WAIT → OFF → WAIT → TRICKLE → CHARGE → HIGH → CHARGE → LOW
b.   WAIT → TRICKLE → WAIT → OFF → WAIT → TRICKLE → CHARGE → LOW → CHARGE
c.   HIGH → CHARGE → LOW → CHARGE → TRICKLE → WAIT → TRICKLE → WAIT → TRICKLE
d.   WAIT → TRICKLE → CHARGE → HIGH → CHARGE → TRICKLE → WAIT → OFF → WAIT In

In State transition testing, a test is defined for each transition. The coverage that is achieved by this testing is called 0-switch. 0-switch coverage is to execute each loop once (No repetition. We should start with initial state and go till end state. It does not test 'sequence of two state transitions').

#TIP: We have only zero switch in foundation level. In Foundation level examination the state transition diagram will be always provided as a part of the question. You just have to follow the given question carefully and pick the right answer.

In this example the start state is 'OFF', and moves following the various transitions & it passes through different states. Remember, in examination the diagram will be provided to you which will help you to understand the question and how to review the question so never get involved in thinking what about other transitions? There could be other valid transition between them? Etc. From the exam point of view pleas stick to the scenario provided. As this is done purposefully to keep you engaged thinking about it and get confused.

Likewise, in this example the question is to find out which of the given option covers maximum transition but not maximum states. So, the easiest way is to quickly draw a rough diagram, pick each option one after the other and start striking the transitions as it covers.

For option A, the path provided is OFF → WAIT → OFF → WAIT → TRICKLE → CHARGE → HIGH → CHARGE → LOW

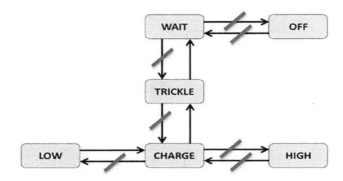

First of all, let's understand that there are total of 10 transition and we need to find the option which covers maximum out of 10 transitions.

As shown in the diagram the above path covers the following transitions. It is also important to recall that, if a transition is repeated as a loop, once a transition is covered, its covered. You don't have to count it twice as it remains the same transition. So, the count here is 7.

Similarly, the option B, will give the count of transition covered by the given path as 7 transitions.

Similarly, the option C, will give the count of transition covered by the given path as 5 transitions.

But when you review option D, this covers 8 transitions out of 10 as shown below.

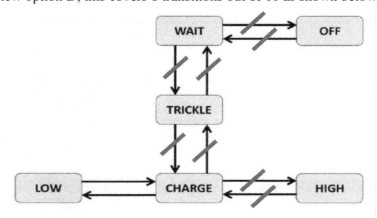

Thus, the correct answer is 'D'

Sample Exam Question:

Given the following state transition table Which of the test cases below will cover the following series of state transitions? S1 SO S1 S2 SO

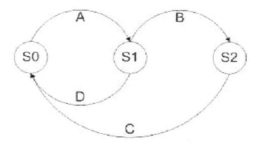

A. D, A, B, C.

B. A, B, C, D.

C. D, A, B.

D. A, B, C.

Let's trace our way through this, our chosen test must cover is:

S1 SO S1 S2 SO

To get from S1 to S0 we have to traverse over Transition D

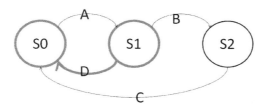

To get from S0 to S1 we have to traverse over Transition A

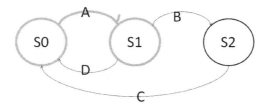

To get from S1 to S2 we have to traverse over Transition B

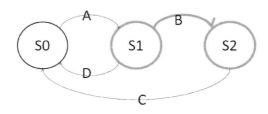

Lastly, to get from S2 to S0 we have to traverse over Transition C

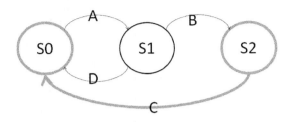

So, the correct answer is DABC, which is option A.

Building Test Cases from state transition diagrams

To build state transition tests that has weakest coverage (visit every state and traverse every transition), use the following method:

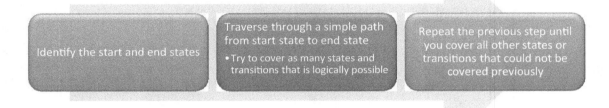

Identify the start and end states

Traverse through a simple path from start state to end state
• Try to cover as many states and transitions that is logically possible

Repeat the previous step until you cover all other states or transitions that could not be covered previously

Developing State Transition Tables

To construct a state transition table:

List all the States in the state transition Diagram

List all the Event[Condition] Combinations

Now, create a table that has a row for each state with every event[condition] combination

Add addional columns for Actions and New States

Complete the table by filling in the Actions and New State Columns

Your table will have the following format:

Current State	Event [Condition]	Action	New State

Let's try this with an example. Consider the state transition diagram below:

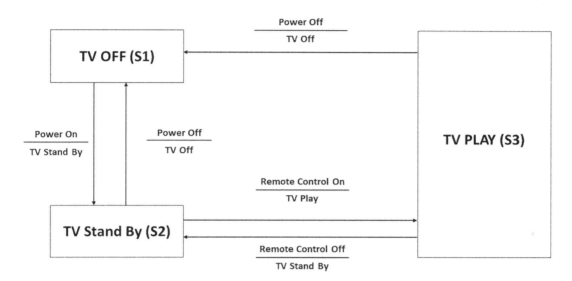

We create a row or entry of each transition shown in the diagram. And each transition shown in the diagram is valid as well as called as a test case. Whereas, as there is no transition between S3 to S1 it is called as Invalid transition.

Our Table will look like this:

Test Case	1	2	3	4	5
Start State	S1	S2	S2	S3	S3
Input	Power On	Power Off	RC On	RC Off	Power Off
Expected Output	TV Stand By	TV Off	TV Play	TV Stand By	TV Off
Final State	S2	S1	S3	S2	S1

SUMMARY ✿
State Transition Testing is applied with help of State Transition Diagram.
State Transition Diagram is pictorial representation of a scenario which shows different STATES and various possible TRANSITIONS between them.
All the transition displayed in diagram are valid or we only represent a valid transition in the diagram.
There must be pair of transition between two states which means both ways. In case the pair is missing the missing transition(s) is called as Invalid
Specifications are basis for applying State Transition Testing.

4.3.5. Use Case Testing (UCT)

Use Case testing is a black box test design technique in which test cases are designed to execute scenarios of use cases.

A use case describes real time interactions between actors and system, where actors are the users. These interactions produce a result of value to a system user or the customer.

A use case can include possible variations of its basic behaviour, including exceptional behaviour and error handling (system response and recovery from programming, application and communication errors, e.g., resulting in an error message). Tests are designed to exercise the defined behaviours (basic, exceptional or alternative, and error handling).

Use cases may be described at the:

- Abstract level
  o Business use case
  o Technology-free
  o Business process level

- System level
  o System use case on the system functionality level

Use Case Sample

Easytravel is a card which is used for paying journeys on buses and undergrounds. The user can store credit to the card at the Easytravel Loading Machines and the system automatically deducts the fee of the journey while the user shows the card to the card reader on a bus or at the underground station.

USE CASE: ADD TO EASYTRAVEL BALANCE FROM CREDIT CARD
Use case ID: UC-201201
Purpose: User is increasing the balance on their Easytravel card.
Actors: user, system
Pre-conditions: User has a valid Easytravel card and a credit card.

Main scenario:

User	System
1. User sets the Easytravel card on the reading plate of the Easytravel Loading Machine.	2. The system asks what the user wishes to do: (E1) a) query card balance (Separate use case) b) add to balance of the card c) check latest card transactions (Separate use case)
3. User chooses "Add balance"	4. System asks the amount. (E1)
5. User selects the amount.	6. System asks for the payment method: (E1) a) cash (Separate use case) b) credit card
7. User selects credit card.	8. System asks the user to insert credit card into the credit card reader. (E1)

9. User inserts the credit card.	10. System shows the amount to be charged from the credit card and asks for confirmation. (E2)
11. User confirms the amount.	12. System makes the credit card transaction and adds the amount to the Easytravel card balance.
13. User removes the credit card and the Easytravel card.	14. System prints out a receipt of the transaction.
	15. System returns to the main screen.

Exceptions:

Exception	Action
E1	User can stop the process by removing the Easytravel card from the reading plate.
E2	If the user does not accept the amount to be charged, they can cancel the operation by pressing the Cancel

End result: User's Easytravel card balance has been increased with the selected amount and the equal amount has been charged to the credit card.

A typical use case:

- Has pre-conditions which need to be met for a use case to work successfully
- Terminates with post-conditions which are the observable results and final state of the system after the use case has been completed
- Has only one mainstream (i.e. a main path) scenario and alternative paths clearly identified.
- For each alternate path there will be separate use cases written for that.
- The exceptions will serve as Invalid test cases.

Use cases describe the "process flows" through a system based on its actual likely use, so the test cases derived from use cases are most useful in uncovering defects in the process flows during real-world use of the system.

Use cases are very useful for designing integration, system testing and acceptance testing. They also help uncover integration defects caused by the interaction and interference of different components, which individual component testing would not see.

Designing test cases from use cases may be combined with other specification-based test techniques such as boundary value analysis, decision table, etc.

SUMMARY ✿
Use cases represent the real-world schedule between the user and the system.
A use case can include possible variations of its basic behaviour, including exceptional behaviour and error handling.
Use cases will always have one main path and all other alternate path clearly identified.
Use cases are helpful for deriving test cases for integration testing, system testing and acceptance testing.
Specifications are basis for applying use cases testing.

4.4. White Box Test Techniques

Structure-based or white-box testing is based on an identified structure of the software or the system, as seen in the following examples:

- At Component level:
  - the structure of single a software component
    - statements eg X = 5
    - decisions eg if X then do Y
    - branches or even distinct paths
- At Integration level:
  - the structure may be a call tree (a diagram in which modules call other modules)
- At System level:
- the structure may be a menu structure, business process or web page structure

In this section, two code-related structural test design techniques for code coverage, based on statements and decisions, are discussed. For decision testing, a control flow diagram may be used to visualize the alternatives for each decision. Both the techniques help to minimize test case for 100% coverage.

4.4.1. Statement Testing or Coverage (SC)

In component testing, statement coverage is the assessment of the percentage of executable statements that have been exercised by a test case suite.

EXECUTABLE STATEMENT: A statement which, when compiled, is translated into object code, and which will be executed procedurally when the program is running and may perform an action on data.

The statement testing technique derives test cases to execute specific statements, normally to increase statement coverage.

Statement coverage is measured as the number of statements executed by the tests divided by the total number of executable statements in the test object, normally expressed as a percentage.

$$Statement\ Coverage = \frac{Number\ of\ Statements\ Executed}{Total\ Number\ of\ Statements} \times 100$$

4.4.2. Decision Testing or Coverage (DC)

Decision coverage, is the assessment of the percentage of decision outcomes (e.g., the True and False options of an IF statement) that have been exercised by a test case suite. The decision testing technique derives test cases to execute specific decision outcomes.

Decision testing can be either called as decision coverage, branch coverage or branch testing.

> **DECISION:** Decision are branches originate from decision points in the code and show the transfer of control to different locations in the code.

Decision coverage is measured as the number of decision outcomes executed by the tests divided by the total number of decision outcomes in the test object, normally expressed as a percentage.

Decision testing is a form of control flow testing as it follows a specific flow of control through the decision points.

$$Decision\ Coverage = \frac{Number\ of\ Decisions\ Executed}{Total\ Number\ of\ Decisions} \times 100$$

Example: Calculating Min. TC for 100% Statement and Decision coverage

Test coverage criteria requires enough test cases such that each condition in a decision takes on all possible outcomes at least once, and each point of entry to a program or subroutine is invoked at least once. That is, every branch (decision) taken each way, true and false. It helps in validating all the branches in the code making sure that no branch leads to abnormal behaviour of the application.

Example:

Calculate statement coverage and decision coverage by analysing the pseudocode below:

Read P
Read Q
IF P+Q > 100 THEN
Print "Large"
ENDIF
If P > 50 THEN
Print "P Large"
ENDIF

Draw the flowchart in the following way -

- Statements, are the activities or printable entities in the code.
- Edges represent non-branching and branching links between nodes.

> #TIP: You may provide with a pseudocode which means it might not be a executable code and is just to express what a code is expected to do. The flow chart is your rough work to derive the right answer.

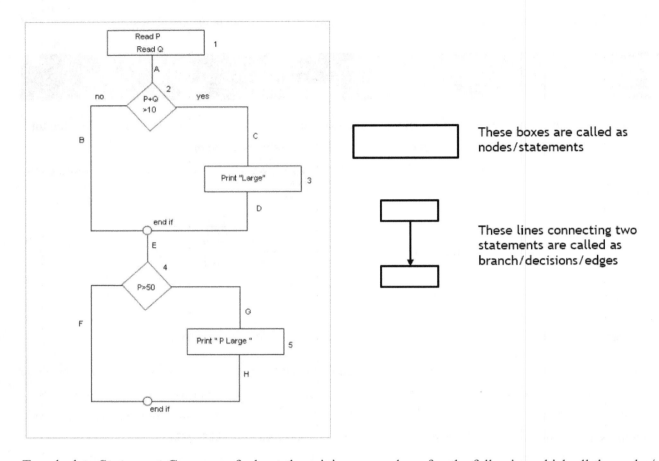

To calculate **Statement Coverage**, find out the minimum number of paths following which all the nodes/ statements will be covered. Here by traversing through path 1A-2C-3D-E-4G-5H all the nodes are covered. So, by traveling through only one path all the nodes 12345 are covered, so the minimum test case required for 100% Statement coverage in this case is 1.

To calculate **Design Coverage**, find out the minimum number of paths which will ensure covering of all the edges. In this case there is no single path which will ensure coverage of all the edges at one go. By following paths 1A-2C-3D-E-4G-5H, maximum numbers of edges (A, C, D, E, G and H) are covered but edges B and F are left. To covers these edges, we can follow 1A-2B-E-4F. By the combining the above two paths we can ensure of traveling through all the paths. Hence, the minimum test case required for 100% Branch Coverage is 2. The aim is to cover all possible true/false decisions.

Thus, for the above example SC=1 and DC=2

SUMMARY ✿

\# Statement Testing or coverage measures all statements with minimum number of TCs.

\# Decision testing or coverage measures all decisions with minimum number of TCs.

\# Decision Testing is stronger technique than Statement Testing. As paths required to test 100% SC may be less than 100% DC for the same code.

\# Decision Testing is also known as Branch Testing.

\# 100% Decision coverage on a code guarantees 100% Statement coverage but not vice-versa.

\# These techniques uses structure, design, code for deriving test cases.

Example Calculating Statement and Decision coverage

For a given fragment of code following paths/test cases have been executed. What statement/ decision coverage is achieved?

Test 1 – A,B,C

Test 2 – A,B,D,F,H

To measure statement coverage, we apply the given formula

$$Statement\ Coverage = \frac{Number\ of\ Statements\ Executed}{Total\ Number\ of\ Statements} \times 100$$

If we apply the given tests on the following control flow diagram, we can conclude that using these tests only Statements A, B, C, D, F & H (which are 6 in count) are covered. Whereas, there are total of 8 statements thus the we have to divide 6/8

Thus, the statement coverage is 75%

To measure decision coverage, we apply the given formula

$$Decision\ Coverage = \frac{Number\ of\ Decisions\ Executed}{Total\ Number\ of\ Decisions} \times 100$$

If we apply the given tests on the following control flow diagram, we can conclude that using these tests only Decisions 1, 2, 3, 6 & 8 (which are 5 in count) are covered. Whereas, there are total of 8 decisions. So, the we have to divide 5/8.

Thus, the decision coverage is 62%

4.5. Experience Based Techniques

Experience-based testing is where tests are derived from the tester's skill and intuition and their experience with similar applications and technologies.

When used to supplement systematic techniques, these techniques can be useful in identifying special tests not easily captured by formal techniques, especially when applied after more formal approaches. However, this technique may yield widely varying degrees of effectiveness, depending on the testers' experience.

These techniques are generally applied after applying formal techniques (such as, black box and white box techniques) to increase the coverage. Sometimes, experience based can only be technique which can be applied. We will see later those scenarios.

4.5.1. Error Guessing

This technique requires knowledge of defects and experience of application. A commonly used experience-based technique is error guessing. Generally, testers anticipate defects based on experience. A structured approach to the error guessing technique is to enumerate a list of possible defects and to design tests that attack these defects. This systematic approach is called *fault attack*. These defect and failure lists can be built based on experience, available defect and failure data, and from common knowledge about why software fails.

Error guessing based on

- How the application has worked in the past
- What types of mistakes the developers tend to make?
- Failures that have occurred in other applications

The reports are formally documented for outcomes and further discussed with test manager for additional efforts.

FAULT ATTACK: An approach where possible defects are identified based on past experience and test are created to uncover these defects.

4.5.2. Exploratory Testing

In exploratory testing, informal (not pre-defined) tests are designed, executed, logged, and evaluated dynamically during test execution. The test results are used to learn more about the component or system, and to create tests for the areas that may need more testing.

Exploratory testing is concurrent test design, test execution, test logging and learning, based on a test charter containing test objectives, and carried out within time-boxes. It is an approach that is most useful where there are few or inadequate specifications and severe time pressure, or in order to augment or complement other, more formal testing.

The approach basically includes allocation of a module to a tester and test it without any pre-orientation and objective. This can result in finding different defects than the one found with formal techniques. It can serve as a check on the test process, to help ensure that the most serious defects are found. Exploratory testing is also useful to complement other more formal testing techniques.

Test charter containing test objectives are the basis to be followed for execution. The execution are *time boxed* with a range between 30 min to 120 min, depending on the size of the application. Executions are called as *test sessions or time boxed test sessions*.

TEST CHARTER: It is document managed for exploratory testing which consist of information like tester name, date, module, time, objective, etc., about the execution.

4.5.3. Checklist Based Testing

In checklist-based testing, testers design, implement, and execute tests to cover test conditions found in a checklist. As part of analysis, testers create a new checklist or expand an existing checklist, but testers may also use an existing checklist without modification. Checklists can be built based on experience, knowledge about what is important for the user, or an understanding of why and how software fails.

In the absence of detailed test cases, checklist-based testing can provide guidelines and a degree of consistency. As these are high-level lists, some variability in the actual testing is likely to occur, resulting in potentially greater coverage but less repeatability.

CHECKLIST: Checklist is an organization level document prepared at organization level containing a questionnaire or list of conditions to be checked while interacting with the product or system.

Quick Revision & Tips on Chapter 4

1. Remember the classification of techniques and categories.
2. Each technique is different from other thus they have different applicability and find different defects from each other.
3. Sample examples will help understand the details of how a technique is applied.
4. K2 level techniques only theory-based questions will be asked.
5. All K3 techniques you have to apply them to derive the right answer.
6. For black box techniques the information about the scenario like ranges, state transition diagram and decision table will be provided in the examination.
7. Similarly, in white box techniques the pseudocode will be given to you (if asked). In new syllabus, they are limited to theory-based question so far. But prepare well.
8. Revise all the summary sections which will enable you to answer few theory based questions.
9. The questions will be specified with which technique to be applied at the last line of question so read carefully before you start solving.
10. Tricky questions are very common in this chapter thus, understand the complete question before you look at the options. Also, read the options twice as just one word can change the meaning of an entire sentence.
11. Quickly revise the bulleted point which would answer most of questions from this chapter.

This chapter will have 11 questions in the examination with following breakup

Chapter 4 Question Distribution	K-Level	Number of Questions per LO	Suggested Points per question	
Keywords	K1	Exactly ONE question based on the definition of a keyword from Chapter 4	1	
FL-4.1.1 **FL-4.2.5** **FL-4.3.1** **FL-4.3.2** **FL-4.3.3** **FL-4.4.1** **FL-4.4.2** **FL-4.4.3**	K2	Exactly FIVE questions based on this set of 8 LOs are required. Each question must cover a DIFFERENT LO. NOTE: Including ONE question for FL-4.2.5 is optional but encouraged.	1	**There is a total of 11 questions required for Chapter 4.** **K1 = 1** **K2 = 5** **K3 = 5** **Number of points for this chapter = 11**
FL-4.2.1 **FL-4.2.2** **FL-4.2.3** **FL-4.2.4**	K3	Exactly FIVE questions based on this set of 4 LOs are required. There shall be ONE question based on EACH of these LOs. (i.e., each question must cover a DIFFERENT LO.) The fifth question shall be based on EITHER FL-4.2.1 OR FL-4.2.2	1	

 # For the exact topic number please refer the ISTQB® official syllabus.

Sample Questions on Chapter 4

1. **In a system designed to work out the tax to be paid: An employee has £4000 of salary tax free. The next £1500 is taxed at 10% The next £28000 is taxed at 22% Any further amount is taxed at 40% Which of these groups of numbers would fall into the same equivalence class?**
   a) £4800; £14000; £28000
   b) £5200; £5500; £28000
   c) £28001; £32000; £35000
   d) £5800; £28000; £32000

2. **What is the expected result for each of the following test cases?**

	Rule 1	Rule 2	Rule 3	Rule 4
Conditions				
Citibank Card Member	Yes	Yes	No	No
Type of Room	Silver	Platinum	Silver	Platinum
Actions				
Offer upgrade to Gold Luxury	Yes	No	No	No
Offer upgrade to Silver	N/A	Yes	N/A	No

   A. Citibank card member, holding a Silver room
   B. Non Citibank-member, holding a Platinum room
   a) A – Don't offer any upgrade, B – Don't offer any upgrade.
   b) A – Don't offer any upgrade, B – Offer upgrade to Gold.
   c) A – Offer upgrade to Silver, B – Offer upgrade to Silver.
   d) A – Offer upgrade to Gold, B – Don't offer any upgrade

3. **Consider the above state transition diagram of a switch. Which of the following represents an invalid state transition?**
   a) OFF to ON
   b) ON to OFF
   c) FAULT to ON
   d) None of the above

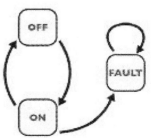

4. Consider the following statements:

   i.   100% statement coverage guarantees 100% branch coverage.

   ii.   100% branch coverage guarantees 100% statement coverage.

   iii.   100% branch coverage guarantees 100% decision coverage.

   iv.   100% decision coverage guarantees 100% branch coverage.

   v.   100% statement coverage guarantees 100% decision coverage.

   a)   ii is True; i, iii, iv & v are False

   b)   i & v are True; ii, iii & iv are False

   c)   ii & iii are True; i, iv & v are False

   d)   ii, iii & iv are True; i & v are False

5. **Minimum Tests Required for Statement Coverage and Branch Coverage:**

   Read P, Read Q

   If p+q > 100 then

   Print "Large"

   End if

   If p > 50 then

   Print "pLarge"

   End if

   a)   Statement coverage is 2 and branch Coverage is 2

   b)   Statement coverage is 3 and branch coverage is 2

   c)   Statement coverage is 1 and branch coverage is 2

   d)   Statement Coverage is 4 and branch coverage is 2

6. **In a flight reservation system, the number of available seats in each plane model is an input. A plane may have any positive number of available seats, up to the given capacity of the plane. Using Boundary Value analysis, a list of available – seat values were generated. Which of the following lists is correct?**

   a)   1, 2, capacity -1, capacity, capacity plus 1

   b)   0, 1, capacity, capacity plus 1

   c)   0, 1, 2, capacity plus 1, a very large number

   d)   0, 1, 10, 100, capacity, capacity plus one

7. **Which of the following is a valid collection of equivalence classes for the following problem: Paying with credit cards shall be possible with Visa, Master and Amex cards only.**

   a)   Visa, Master, Amex;

   b)   Visa, Master, Amex, Diners, Keycards, and other option

   c)   Visa, Master, Amex, any other card, no card

   d)   No card, other cards, any of Visa – Master – Amex

8. Which of the options below would be the BEST basis for testing using fault attacks?

a) Experience, defect and failure data; knowledge about software failures

b) Risk identification performed at the beginning of the project

c) Use Cases derived from business flows by domain experts

d) Expected results from comparison with an existing system

9. You are working on a project that has poor specifications and time pressure. Which of the following test techniques would be the best test approach to use?

a) Use Case Testing

b) Statement Testing

c) Exploratory Testing

d) Decision Testing

10. Which of the following options lists techniques categorized as Black Box design techniques?

a) Equivalence Partitioning, Decision Table testing, State Transition testing, and Boundary Value analysis

b) Equivalence Partitioning, Decision Table testing, Statement coverage, Use Case Based testing

c) Equivalence Partitioning, Decision Coverage testing, Use Case Based testing

d) Equivalence Partitioning, Decision Coverage testing, Boundary Value analysis

Answer to the questions can be found at the last page of the book

Chapter 5

Test Management

5. Test Management

Terms: Configuration management, Defect management, Entry criteria, Exit criteria, Product risk, Project risk, Risk, Risk level, Risk-based testing, Test approach, Test control, Test estimation, Test manager, Tester, Test monitoring, Test plan, Test planning, Test progress report, Test strategy, Test summary report.

5.1. Test Organization

5.1.1. Independent Testing

The effectiveness of finding defects by testing and reviews can be improved by using independent testers. Independent testing means a piece of code being tested by a person other than who wrote the code. Now, the degree of this independent tester may vary depending on different conditions and for different levels. We experience various degree of independence across organisation. When summarised, independence include the following (moving from lowest to highest):

- No independent testers; developers test their own code
- Independent testers within the development teams
- Independent test team or group within the organization, reporting to project management or executive management
- Independent testers from the business organization or user community, test specialists for specific test types such as usability testers, security testers or certification testers (who certify a software product against standards and regulations)
- Independent testers outsourced or external to the organization

For large, complex or safety critical projects, it is usually best to have multiple levels of testing, with some or all of the levels done by independent testers. Development staff may participate in testing, especially at the lower levels, but their lack of objectivity often limits their effectiveness. The independent testers may have the authority to require and define test processes and rules, but testers should take on such process-related roles only in the presence of a clear management mandate to do so.

An organisation may practice any of these degrees or may be all of them at different test levels. E.g. Unit test may have 2nd degree where another developer within the same development team can test the code whereas, performance testing can be outsourced as mention in 5th degree.

There are benefits and drawbacks at both the ends for least independent as well as highest independent testers. But, by summarizing we understand that least independent testers may not be able to find different defects as highly independent team can. Based on this understanding let's see what are the key benefits and drawbacks of independent testing as overall.

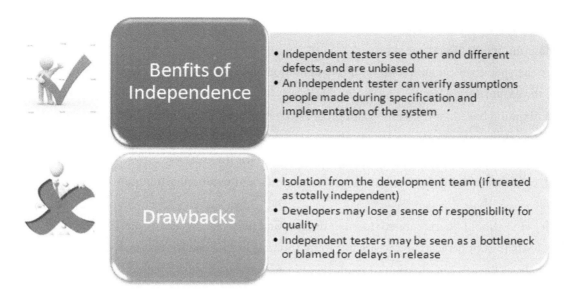

Benefits of Independence
- Independent testers see other and different defects, and are unbiased
- An independent tester can verify assumptions people made during specification and implementation of the system

Drawbacks
- Isolation from the development team (if treated as totally independent)
- Developers may lose a sense of responsibility for quality
- Independent testers may be seen as a bottleneck or blamed for delays in release

5.1.2. Task of a Test Manager and Tester

In this syllabus two test positions are covered, test manager and tester.

The activities and tasks performed by people in these two roles depend on the project and product context, the people in the roles, and the organization.

Sometimes the test manager is called a test leader or test coordinator. The role of the test manager may be performed by a project manager, a development manager, a quality assurance manager or the manager of a test group.

In larger projects two positions may exist: test leader and test manager. Typically, the test leader plans, monitors and controls the testing activities and tasks as defined in chapter 1.

TEST MANAGER: The person responsible for project management of testing activities and resources, and evaluation of a test object. The individual who directs, controls, administers, plans and regulates the evaluation of a test object.

Typical tasks of a Test Manager may include ❀

- Coordinate the test strategy and plan with project managers and others.
- Write or review a test strategy for the project, and test policy for the organization.
- Contribute the testing perspective to other project activities, such as integration planning.

- Plan the tests – considering the context and understanding the test objectives and risks – including:
  - selecting test approaches
  - estimating the time
  - effort and cost of testing
  - acquiring resources
  - defining test levels and cycles
  - planning incident management
- Initiate the specification, preparation, implementation and execution of tests, monitor the test results and check the exit criteria.
- Adapt planning based on test results and progress (sometimes documented in status reports) and take any action necessary to compensate for problems.
- Set up adequate configuration management of testware for traceability
- Introduce suitable metrics for measuring test progress and evaluating the quality of the testing and the product
- Decide what should be automated, to what degree, and how
- Select tools to support testing and organize any training in tool use for testers
- Decide about the implementation of the test environment
- Write test summary reports based on the information gathered during testing
- Promote and advocate the testers, the test team, and the test profession within the organization
- Develop the skills and careers of testers (e.g., through training plans, performance evaluations, coaching, etc.)

TESTER: A skilled professional who is involved in the testing of a component or system. Additionally, responsible for preparing and executing test cases.

Typical tasks of a Tester may include:

- Review and contribute to test plans
- Analyse, review and assess user requirements, specifications and models for testability
- Create test specifications
- Set up the test environment (often coordinating with system administration and network management)
- Prepare and acquire test data
- Create the detailed test execution schedule
- Implement tests on all test levels, execute and log the tests, evaluate the results and document the deviations from expected results
- Use test administration or management tools and test monitoring tools as required
- Automate tests (may be supported by a developer or a test automation expert)
- Evaluate non-functional characteristics such as performance efficiency, reliability, usability, security, compatibility, and portability
- Review tests developed by others

People who work on test analysis, test design, specific test types or test automation may be specialists in these roles. Depending on the test level and the risks related to the product and the project, different people may take over the role of tester, keeping some degree of independence.

Typically, testers at the component and integration level would be developers, testers at the acceptance test level would be business experts and users, and testers for operational acceptance testing would be operators.

5.2. Test Planning and Estimation

5.2.1. Purpose and Content of a Test Plan

This section covers the purpose of test planning within development and implementation projects, and for maintenance activities.

The Planning maybe documented in a master test plan and in separate test plans for test levels such as system testing and acceptance testing.

Planning is influenced by:

- the test policy of the organization
- the scope of testing
- objectives
- risks
- constraints
- criticality
- testability and the availability of resources.

As the project and test planning progress, more information becomes available and more detail can be included in the plan. Feedback from test activities is used to recognize changing risks so that planning can be adjusted.

Test planning is a continuous activity and is managed throughout the testing lifecycle. Depending on the ongoing monitoring activities a test plan can be updated by test manager.

There are four major documents in a test organization and these are prepared by test manager.

Test Policy – An organization level document which mainly describes the organization's practices and assets about testing. These are quite commonly created in a service-based organization.

Test Strategy – A document which is project specific and have detailed approach for the project. Some organisation may include their strategy within the test plan document. For product-based organization it may remain same as they work on a common product every time.

Master Test Plan – This is the Test plan document which describes the detailed list of different activities which will be conducted as a part of testing lifecycle.

Level Test Plan – This is another document which consist of similar activities to that of test plan for a test level. This will be separately created for each test level to be performed.

We have learnt the test planning and related activities of this phase in chapter 1. Let's quickly recap the same. Test planning activities may include the following and some of these may be documented in a test plan:

- Determining the scope, objectives, and risks of testing
- Defining the overall approach of testing
- Integrating and coordinating the test activities into the software lifecycle activities
- Making decisions about what to test, the people and other resources required to perform the various test activities, and how test activities will be carried out
- Scheduling of test analysis, design, implementation, execution, and evaluation activities, either on particular dates (e.g., in sequential development) or in the context of each iteration (e.g., in iterative development)
- Selecting metrics for test monitoring and control
- Budgeting for the test activities
- Determining the level of detail and structure for test documentation (e.g., by providing templates or example documents)

5.2.2. Test Strategy and Test Approach

The test approach:

- Is the implementation of the test strategy for a specific project
- Is defined and refined in the test plans and test designs
- It typically includes the decisions made based on the (test) project's goal and risk assessment.
- It is the starting point for planning the test process, for selecting the test design techniques and test types to be applied, and for defining the entry and exit criteria

The selected approach depends on the context and may consider risks, hazards and safety, available resources and skills, the technology, the nature of the system (e.g., custom built vs. COTS), test objectives, and regulations.

Typical approaches include:

- **Analytical**: This type of test strategy is based on an analysis of some factor (e.g., requirement or risk). Risk-based testing is an example of an analytical approach, where tests are designed and prioritized based on the level of risk.
- **Model-Based**: In this type of test strategy, tests are designed based on some model of some required aspect of the product, such as a function, a business process, an internal structure, or a non-functional characteristic (e.g., reliability). Examples of such models include business process models, state models, and reliability growth models.
- **Methodical**: This type of test strategy relies on making systematic use of some predefined set of tests or test conditions, such as a taxonomy of common or likely types of failures, a list of important quality characteristics, or company-wide look-and-feel standards for mobile apps or web pages.

- **Process-compliant (or standard-compliant)**: This type of test strategy involves analysing, designing, and implementing tests based on external rules and standards, such as those specified by industry-specific standards, by process documentation, by the rigorous identification and use of the test basis, or by any process or standard imposed on or by the organization.

- **Directed (or consultative)**: This type of test strategy is driven primarily by the advice, guidance, or instructions of stakeholders, business domain experts, or technology experts, who may be outside the test team or outside the organization itself.

- **Regression-averse**: This type of test strategy is motivated by a desire to avoid regression of existing capabilities. This test strategy includes reuse of existing testware (especially test cases and test data), extensive automation of regression tests, and standard test suites.

- **Reactive**: In this type of test strategy, testing is reactive to the component or system being tested, and the events occurring during test execution, rather than being pre-planned (as the preceding strategies are). Tests are designed and implemented, and may immediately be executed in response to knowledge gained from prior test results. Exploratory testing is a common technique employed in reactive strategies.

Different approaches may be combined, for example, a risk-based dynamic approach.

> You don't have to worry about getting into the details of these approaches as details are covered in Test Analyst (Advance Level. Question will be related to the content here(If any).

5.2.3. Entry Criteria and Exit Criteria (Definition of Ready and Definition of Done)

As part of test planning, we learnt that we create Entry and Exit Criteria. These are basically certain list of criteria, to do list or a simple checklist which determines when to start or end a phase in test lifecycle or for test lifecycle as well. It's as simple as a list of grocery which you have to manage or purchase in order to prepare a delicious dish. Entry and Exist criteria can be used for a project as well as internally within other phase of a development model like development, design, etc.

Entry criteria, is a list of preconditions which are supposed to be performed before getting into or getting started with a particular phase in testing. In case, entry criteria are not met, we try to complete the pending activities in list first before starting the activity it is designed for. Entry criteria in agile methodology is commonly known as *definition of ready*.

Similarly, Exit criteria, is a list of postconditions which are supposed to be performed before closing or calling off a particular phase in testing. In case, exit criteria is not met, we target the desired steps to achieve the defined activities in list first before calling the test phase complete. Exit criteria in agile methodology is commonly known as *definition of done*.

Following are the typical examples of entry and exit criteria. This may vary from organization to organization and project to project.

Typically, entry criteria may cover the following:

Avalability of requirement, users storeis, etc.

Test tool readiness in the test environment

Testable code availability

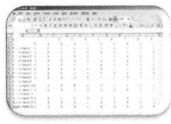

Test data availability

Test environment availability and readiness

Typically exit criteria may cover the following:

Thoroughness measures, such as coverage of code, functionality or risk

Estimates of defect density or reliability measures

Number of unresolved defects is in agreed limit

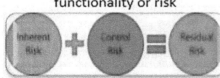

Residual risks, such as defects not fixed or lack of test coverage in certain areas

Planned tests have been completed as planned

Evaluated levels of quliaity characteristics.

Even without exit criteria being satisfied, it is also common for test activities to be curtailed due to the budget being expended, the scheduled time being completed, and/or pressure to bring the product to market. It can be acceptable to end testing under such circumstances, if the project stakeholders and business owners have reviewed and accepted the risk to go live without further testing.

5.2.4. Test Execution Schedule

Once the various test cases and test procedures are produced (with some test procedures potentially automated) and assembled into test suites, the test suites can be arranged in a test execution schedule that defines the order in which they are to be run. The test execution schedule should take into account such factors as prioritization, dependencies, confirmation tests, regression tests, and identify the most efficient sequence for executing the tests.

Ideally, test cases would be ordered to run based on their priority levels, usually by executing the test cases with the highest priority first. However, this practice may not work if the test cases have dependencies or the features being tested have dependencies.

Let's understand this in better and simple way. If a test case with a higher priority is dependent on a test case with a lower priority, the lower priority test case must be executed first. Similarly, if there are dependencies across test cases, they must be ordered appropriately regardless of their relative priorities. Confirmation and regression tests must be prioritized as well, based on the importance of rapid feedback on changes, but here again dependencies may apply.

Here is an example to understand the same. Consider the following table below

Test Case	Priority	Technical Dependency	Logical Dependency
TC1	High	TC4	
TC2	Low		
TC3	High		TC4
TC4	Medium		
TC5	Low		TC2
TC6	Medium	TC5	

In this example, based on priority the sequence of execution is TC1-> TC3 -> TC4 -> TC6 -> TC2 ->TC5. But if we further consider the technical and logical dependency, we see test cases have further dependency on other test cases.

Here, TC1 and TC3 both having high priority but being dependent on TC4. Thus, TC4 having medium priority will be executed before TC1 and TC3. Similarly, TC6 having medium priority should be executed before low priority but, TC6 is dependent on TC5 and TC5 is further dependent on TC2. Thus, TC2 being having lowest priority will be executed before TC6.

So, the final order of execution will be TC4 -> TC1 ->TC3 -> TC2 -> TC5 -> TC6.

5.2.5. Test Estimation Techniques

Test estimation, being a management activity is an approach to measure the required time, cost and effort for each testing activity. This is generally a task of Test Manager. The best estimates:

- Represent the collective wisdom of experienced practitioners and have the support of the participants involved
- Provide specific, detailed catalogs of the costs, resources, tasks, and people involved
- Present, for each activity estimated, the most likely cost, effort and duration

Though test estimation is a management activity it may involve other team members to contribute in estimation sessions. This not only helps everyone understand the estimates also help to involve different perception for better and precise estimation.

As this involves major responsibility of Test Manager this topic is discussed in more details at advance level syllabus. In foundation, we are targeting a basic introduction so that we are aware of various activities within test organisation.

In this syllabus, we are limited to understand what are the different techniques for test estimation. Two approaches for the estimation of test effort are:

- The **metrics-based approach**: estimating the testing effort based on metrics of former or similar projects or based on typical values
- The **expert-based approach**: estimating the tasks based on estimates made by the owner of the tasks or by experts

For example, in Agile development, burndown charts are examples of the metrics-based approach as effort is being captured and reported, and is then used to feed into the team's velocity to determine the amount of work the team can do in the next iteration; whereas planning poker is an example of the expert-based approach, as team members are estimating the effort to deliver a feature based on their experience.

Within sequential projects, defect removal models are examples of the metrics-based approach, where volumes of defects and time to remove them are captured and reported, which then provides a basis for estimating future projects of a similar nature; whereas the Wideband Delphi estimation technique is an example of the expert-based approach in which groups of experts provides estimates based on their experience.

Once the test effort is estimated, resources can be identified and a schedule can be drawn up.

5.2.6. Factors Influencing the Test Efforts

Test effort estimation involves predicting the amount of test-related work that will be needed in order to meet the objectives of the testing for a particular project, release, or iteration. Factors influencing the test effort may include characteristics of the product, characteristics of the development process, characteristics of the people, and the test results, as shown below.

Product Characteristics

- The risks associated with the product (based on risk analysis)
- The quality of the test basis (detailed or brief)
- The size of the product
- The complexity of the product domain
- The requirements for quality characteristics (e.g., security, reliability)
- The required level of detail for test documentation (e.g. Agile has minimal documentation)
- Requirements for legal and regulatory compliance

Development Process Characteristics

- The stability and maturity of the organization (CMM Level maturity)
- The development model in use
- The test approaches (test strategy)
- The tools used (to support automation, test execution, test management)
- The test process
- Time pressure (in case of agile)

People Characteristics

- The skills and experience of the people involved, especially with similar projects and products (e.g., domain knowledge)
- Team cohesion and leadership

Test Results

- The number and severity of defects found
- The amount of rework required

5.3. Test Monitoring and Control

The purpose of test monitoring is to provide feedback and visibility about test activities. Information to be monitored may be collected manually or automatically and may be used to measure exit criteria, such as coverage. This activity is generally done with help of metrics.

> **TEST MONITORING:** It is process of measuring progress on the project which is done with help of several metrics which are helpful in measuring any activity across the project.

Test control describes any guiding or corrective actions taken as a result of information and metrics gathered and reported. Actions may cover any test activity and may affect any other software life cycle activity or task.

Examples of test control actions include:

- Making decisions based on information from test monitoring

- Re-prioritizing tests when an identified risk occurs e.g., software delivered late

- Changing the test schedule due to availability or unavailability of a test environment

> Setting an entry criterion requiring fixes to have been re-tested (confirmation tested) by a developer before accepting them into a build

*For an example, if you are driving to a place which is unknown to you. We generally take help of maps and try to follow the route while we drive to reach our destination. Here, consistently following the direction on maps is referred to **Monitoring**. Map tracking your movement with respect to the direction on the maps is a **Metric**. In case you take a wrong deviation, map tries to re-route and give you a new path or sometimes asks you to go back a bit and follow the earlier determined path, this is referred as **Control Action.***

5.3.1. Metrics used in Testing

Metrics are certain set of calculations or formulae which helps us to measure a process or progress on an activity within a process.

Metrics can be collected during and at the end of test activities in order to assess:

- Progress against the planned schedule and budget
- Current quality of the test object
- Adequacy of the test approach
- Effectiveness of the test activities with respect to the objectives

Common test metrics include:

- Percentage of planned work done in test case preparation (or percentage of planned test cases implemented)
- Percentage of planned work done in test environment preparation
- Test case execution (e.g., number of test cases run/not run, test cases passed/failed, and/or test conditions passed/failed)
- Defect information (e.g., defect density, defects found and fixed, failure rate, and confirmation test results)
- Test coverage of requirements, user stories, acceptance criteria, risks, or code
- Task completion, resource allocation and usage, and effort
- Cost of testing, including the cost compared to the benefit of finding the next defect or the cost compared to the benefit of running the next test

For example, if we consider Test Case Execution it is measured as

$$Test\ Case\ Execution\ Rate = \frac{Number\ of\ Test\ Cases\ Executed}{Total\ Number\ Test\ Cases\ Planned\ for\ Execution} \times 100$$

In similar way all other metrics are measurable.

5.3.2. Purposes, Contents and Audiences for Test Report

Test reporting is concerned with summarizing information about the testing endeavour, including:

- What happened during a period of testing, such as milestone dates, etc.
- Analysed information and metrics to support recommendations and decisions about future actions, such as an assessment of defects remaining, the economic benefit of continued testing, outstanding risks, and the level of confidence in the tested software

The purpose of test reporting is to summarize and communicate test activity information, both during and at the end of a test activity (e.g., a test level). The test report prepared during a test activity may be referred to as a ***test progress report***, while a test report is prepared at the end of a test life cycle containing the summary of all major activities conducted throughout may be referred to as a ***test summary report***.

During test monitoring and control, the test manager regularly issues test progress reports for stakeholders. In addition to content common to test progress reports and test summary reports, typical test progress reports may also include:

- The status of the test activities and progress against the test plan
- Factors impeding progress
- Testing planned for the next reporting period
- The quality of the test object

When exit criteria are reached, the test manager issues the test summary report. This report provides a summary of the testing performed, based on the latest test progress report and any other relevant information. Typical **test progress reports** and **test summary reports** may include:

- Summary of testing performed
- Information on what occurred during a test period
- Deviations from plan, including deviations in schedule, duration, or effort of test activities
- Status of testing and product quality with respect to the exit criteria or definition of done
- Factors that have blocked or continue to block progress
- Metrics of defects, test cases, test coverage, activity progress, and resource consumption.
- Residual risks
- Reusable test work products produced

The contents of a test report will vary depending on the project, the organizational requirements, and the software development lifecycle. For example, a complex project with many stakeholders or a regulated project may require more detailed and rigorous reporting than a quick software update. As another example, in Agile development, test progress reporting may be incorporated into task boards, defect summaries, and burndown charts, which may be discussed during a daily stand-up meeting

5.4. Configuration Management

Configuration Management, alternatively known as ***Version Control*** is a management of history or revision done on any entity. The purpose of configuration management is to establish and maintain the integrity of the products (components, data and documentation) of the software or system throughout the project and product life cycle.

This management will help us identify the new version and will also assist in determining the changes done which can be helpful in determining effort for subsequent activities which follows.

For testing, configuration management may involve ensuring the following:

- All items of testware are identified, version controlled, tracked for changes, related to each other and related to development items (test objects) so that traceability can be maintained throughout the test process
- All identified documents and software items are referenced unambiguously in test documentation

The configuration management procedures and infrastructure (tools) should be chosen, documented and implemented during test planning. As the revision of test plan may also happen it requires the implementation of configuration management much earlier in the lifecycle.

For an instance, if a requirement is modified then we can have a quick comparison between the old and new version of the document to determine if additional test cases are required to be written or the existing will suffice.

5.5. Risk and Testing

5.5.1. Definition of Risk

Before we understand the definition, let's be clear about this topic. This topic is about Risk and Testing and we are talking about basics of Risk Based Testing (Analytical approach), whereas the detailed approach is different. Here, we will understand what is risk and what are different types of risk in testing with examples.

Risk can be defined as the chance of an event, hazard, threat or situation occurring and resulting in undesirable consequences or a potential problem. Alternatively, can also be said that, a risk is an predicted uncertainty which may or may not happen.

The level of risk will be determined by the likelihood of an adverse event to happen (Probability) and the impact (the harm resulting from that event).

This syllabus targets two types of risk

- Project Risk (Impacts the process/project)
- Product Risk (Impacts the end user of product)

5.5.2. Project and Product Risk

Project Risks ✿

Project risk involves situations that, should they occur, may have a negative effect on a project's ability to achieve its objectives. These are related to activities performed within a project or development lifecycle. Project risk can be associated to communication, co-ordination, documentation, etc. Examples of project risks include:

> **PROJECT RISK:** Project risk is any such uncertainty which may impact the process of making a product or system which in simple terms means a project risk. These are internal risks which take place before release and may obstruct the successful release.

- Project issues:
  - o Delays may occur in delivery, task completion, or satisfaction of exit criteria or definition of done
  - o Inaccurate estimates, reallocation of funds to higher priority projects, or general cost-cutting across the organization may result in inadequate funding
  - o Late changes may result in substantial re-work

- Organizational issues:
  - o Skills, training, and staff may not be sufficient
  - o Personnel issues may cause conflict and problems
  - o Users, business staff, or subject matter experts may not be available due to conflicting business priorities

- Political issues:
  - o Testers may not communicate their needs and/or the test results adequately
  - o Developers and/or testers may fail to follow up on information found in testing and reviews (e.g., not improving development and testing practices)
  - o There may be an improper attitude toward, or expectations of, testing (e.g., not appreciating the value of finding defects during testing)

- Technical issues:
  - o Requirements may not be defined well enough
  - o The requirements may not be met, given existing constraints

- The test environment may not be ready on time
- Data conversion, migration planning, and their tool support may be late
- Weaknesses in the development process may impact the consistency or quality of project work products such as design, code, configuration, test data, and test cases
- Poor defect management and similar problems may result in accumulated defects and other technical debt

- Supplier issues:
  - A third party may fail to deliver a necessary product or service, or go bankrupt
  - Contractual issues may cause problems to the project

Product Risks ✤

Product risks are the risks that are directly related to the test object.

Potential failure areas (adverse future events or hazards) in the software or system are known as product risks, as they are a risk to the quality of the product. Thus, they are also called as quality risks. These risks are generally associated with work products, quality characteristics, behaviour, etc of the products.

> **PRODUCT RISK:** Product risk is any such uncertainty which may impact or harm the end user of the product or system. These are external risks which takes place after release.

These include:

- Software might not perform its intended functions according to the specification
- Software might not perform its intended functions according to user, customer, and/or stakeholder needs
- A system architecture may not adequately support some non-functional requirement(s)
- A particular computation may be performed incorrectly in some circumstances
- A loop control structure may be coded incorrectly
- Response-times may be inadequate for a high-performance transaction processing system
- User experience (UX) feedback might not meet product expectations

5.5.3. Risk Based Testing and Product Quality

Risks are used to decide where to start testing and where to test more; testing is used to reduce the risk of an adverse effect occurring, or to reduce the impact of an adverse effect. Testing as a risk-control activity provides feedback about the residual risk by measuring the effectiveness of critical defect removal and of contingency plans.

A risk-based approach to testing provides proactive opportunities to reduce the levels of product risk, starting in the initial stages of a project. It involves the identification of product risks and their use in guiding test planning and control, specification, preparation and execution of tests.

In a risk-based approach the risks identified may be used to:

- Determine the test techniques to be employed
- Determine the extent of testing to be carried out
- Prioritize testing in an attempt to find the critical defects as early as possible
- Determine whether any non-testing activities could be employed to reduce risk (e.g., providing training to inexperienced designers)

Risk-based testing draws on the collective knowledge and insight of the project stakeholders to determine the risks and the levels of testing required to address those risks.

To ensure that the chance of a product failure is minimized, risk management activities provide a disciplined approach to:

- Assess (and reassess on a regular basis) what can go wrong (risks)
- Determine what risks are important to deal with
- Implement actions to deal with those risks

In addition, testing may support the identification of new risks, may help to determine what risks should be reduced, and may lower uncertainty about risks.

5.6. Defect Management

Since one of the objectives of testing is to find defects, the discrepancies between actual and expected outcomes need to be logged as defects.

A defect shall be investigated further for validity as it's possible that a defect may have been raised as a misunderstanding of a tester. Once validated, appropriate actions to fix defects shall be defined. Defects shall be tracked from the point of identification and classification to correction and confirmation of the solution.

In order to manage all defects, an organization should establish a defect management process and rules for classification.

A defect may be raised during development, review, testing or use of a software product. They may be raised for issues in code or the working system, or in any type of documentation including requirements, development documents, test documents, and user information such as "Help" or installation guides.

Defects reports have the following objectives:

- Provide developers and other parties with feedback about the problem to enable identification, isolation and correction as necessary
- Provide test leaders a means of tracking the quality of the system under test and the progress of the testing
- Provide ideas for test process improvement

Details of the defect report may include:

- Date of issue, issuing organization, and author
- Expected and actual results
- Identification of the test item (configuration item) and environment
- Software or system life cycle process in which the incident was observed
- Description of the incident to enable reproduction and resolution, including logs, database dumps or screenshots
- Severity of the impact on the system
- Urgency/priority to fix
- Status of the incident (e.g., open, deferred, duplicate, waiting to be fixed, fixed awaiting re-test, closed)
- Conclusions, recommendations and approvals
- Global issues, such as other areas that may be affected by a change resulting from the incident
- Change history, such as the sequence of actions taken by project team members with respect to the incident to isolate, repair, and confirm it as fixed
- References, including the identity of the test case specification that revealed the problem

Quick Revision & Tips on Chapter 5

1. Benefits and drawbacks of independent testing are important.
2. Understand the difference between the Role of a Tester and Test Manager. Remember the activities performed by them.
3. For test strategy, typically knowing the approaches are good. But, rarely seen with a question.
4. Mainly a question on activities of Test planning may appear here
5. Understand the core difference between entry and exit criteria. Typically, the question is given with set of examples and asked to pick the entry and exit or Criterion
6. For test estimation the types are enough to be remembered. The factors influencing test effort may be add on.
7. Should recall the test execution schedule and understand the dependency
8. Product risk and project Risk are different. Example of the same will be helpful.
9. In defect management the key area to concentrate is the objective and the important details of defect Report.
10. It's possible that you can expect one question using NOT or FALSE.
11. Quickly revise the bulleted point which would answer most of questions from this chapter.

This chapter will have 9 questions in the examination with following breakup

Chapter 5 Question Distribution	K-Level	Number of Questions per LO	Suggested Points per question	
FL-5.1.2 FL-5.2.5 FL-5.3.1 FL=5.5.1	K1	Exactly TWO questions based on this set of 4 LOs are required. Each question must cover a DIFFERENT LO.	1	**There is a total of 9 questions required for Chapter 5.** **K1 = 2** **K2 = 5** **K3 = 2** **Number of points for this chapter = 9**
FL-5.1.1 FL-5.2.1 FL-5.2.2 FL-5.2.3 FL-5.2.6 FL-5.3.2 FL-5.4.1 FL-5.5.2 FL-5.5.3	K2	Exactly FIVE questions based on this set of 9 LOs are required. Each question must cover a DIFFERENT LO.	1	
FL-5.2.4 FL-5.6.1	K3	Exactly TWO questions based on this set of two LOs is required. Each question must cover a DIFFERENT LO.	1	

 # For the exact topic number please refer the ISTQB® official syllabus.

Sample Questions on Chapter 5

1. **Which of the following BEST describes how tasks are divided between the test manager and the tester?**
   a) The test manager plans testing activities and chooses the standards to be followed, while the tester chooses the tools and controls to be used.
   b) The test manager plans, organizes, and controls the testing activities, while the tester specifies and executes tests.
   c) The test manager plans, monitors, and controls the testing activities, while the tester designs tests and decides about the approval of the test object.
   d) The test manager plans and organizes the testing, and specifies the test cases, while the tester prioritizes and executes the tests.

2. **What information need NOT be included in a test incident report:**
   a) how to fix the fault
   b) how to reproduce the fault
   c) test environment details
   d) severity, priority

3. **Which of the following is NOT included in the Test Plan document of the Test Documentation Standard:**
   a) Test items (i.e. software versions)
   b) What is not to be tested
   c) Test environments
   d) Schedules

4. **The following list contains risks that have been identified for a software product to be developed. Which of these risks is an example of a product risk?**
   a) Not enough qualified testers to complete the planned tests
   b) Software delivery is behind schedule
   c) Threat to a patient's life
   d) 3rd party supplier does not supply as stipulated

5. **Which set of metrics can be used for monitoring of the test execution?**
   a) Number of detected defects, testing cost;
   b) Number of residual defects in the test object.
   c) Percentage of completed tasks in the preparation of test environment; test cases prepared
   d) Number of test cases run / not run; test cases passed / failed

6. **From a Testing perspective, what are the MAIN purposes of Configuration Management?**
   i) **Identifying the version of software under test.**
   ii) **Controlling the version of testware items.**
   iii) **Developing new testware items.**
   iv) **Tracking changes to testware items.**
   v) **Analysing the need for new testware items.**
   a) ii, iv and v.
   b) ii, iii and iv.
   c) i, ii and iv.
   d) i, iii and v.

7. **What is the purpose of test exit criteria in the test plan?**
   a) To specify when to stop the testing activity
   b) To set the criteria used in generating test inputs
   c) To ensure that the test case specification is complete
   d) To know when a specific test has finished its execution

8. **Benefits of Independent Testing**
   a) Independent testers are much more qualified than Developers
   b) Independent testers see other and different defects and are unbiased.
   c) Independent Testers cannot identify defects.
   d) Independent Testers can test better than developers

9. **Which of the following is a project risk?**
   a) Skill and staff shortages
   b) Poor software characteristics (e.g. usability)
   c) Failure-prone software delivered
   d) Possible reliability defect (bug)

10. **As a test manager, you are asked for a test summary report. Concerning test activities, and according to the IEEE 829 Standard, what should be the MOST important information to include in your report?**
    a) The number of test cases executed and their results.
    b) An overview of the major testing activities, events and the status with respect to meeting goals
    c) Overall evaluation of each development work item
    d) Training taken by members of the test team to support the test effort

Answer to the questions can be found at the last page of the book

Chapter 6

Tool Support for Testing

6. Tool Support for Testing

Terms: Data-driven testing, Keyword-driven testing, Performance testing tool, Test automation, Test execution tool, Test management tool

6.1. Test Tool Considerations

6.1.1. Meaning and Purpose of Test Tools

Test tools are any independent application which serves testing directly or indirectly. These tools can aid testing support either by managing resources or executing tests automatically. Test tools can be used for one or more activities that support testing. These include:

1. Tools that are directly used in testing such as:
    a. Test execution tools
    b. Test data generation tools
    c. Result comparison tools
2. Tools that help in managing the testing process such as those used to manage:
    a. Tests
    b. Test results
    c. Test data
    d. Requirements
    e. Defects
    f. Reporting and monitoring
3. Tools that are used in reconnaissance, or, in simple terms: exploration. Examples include:
    a. Tools that monitor file activity for an application
4. Any tool that aids in testing (example a spreadsheet is also a test tool in this meaning)

Tool support for testing can have one or more of the following purposes depending on the context:

*   Improve the efficiency of test activities by automating repetitive tasks or supporting manual test activities like test planning, test design, test reporting and monitoring

- Automate activities that require significant resources when done manually (e.g., static testing)
- Automate activities that cannot be executed manually (e.g., large scale performance testing of client-server applications)
- Increase reliability of testing (e.g., by automating large data comparisons or simulating behaviour)

6.1.2. Test Tool Classification

There are a number of tools that support different aspects of testing.

Tools can be classified based on several criteria such as:

- Purpose
- Commercial / free / open-source / shareware
- Technology etc.

Tools are classified in this syllabus according to the testing activities that they support. Some tools clearly support one activity; others may support more than one activity, but are classified under the activity with which they are most closely associated.

Tools from a single provider, especially those that have been designed to work together, may be bundled into one package.

Some types of test tool can be intrusive, which means that they can affect the actual outcome of the test.

For example, the actual timing may be different due to the extra instructions that are executed by the tool, or you may get a different measure of code coverage.

The consequence of intrusive tools is called the probe effect.

Some tools offer support more appropriate for developers (e.g., tools that are used during component and component integration testing). Such tools are marked with "(D)" in the list below.

Tool Support for Management of Testing and Tests

Management tools may apply to any test activities over the entire software development lifecycle. Examples of tools that support management of testing and testware include:

Test Management Tools	These tools provide interfaces for executing tests, tracking defects and managing requirements, along with support for quantitative analysis and reporting of the test objects. They also support tracing the test objects to requirement specifications and might have an independent version control capability or an interface to an external one.
Requirement Management Tools	These tools store requirement statements, store the attributes for the requirements (including priority), provide unique identifiers and support tracing the requirements to individual tests. These tools may also help with identifying inconsistent or missing requirements.

Defect Management Tools	These tools store and manage incident reports, i.e. defects, failures, change requests or perceived problems and anomalies, and help in managing the life cycle of incidents, optionally with support for statistical analysis.
Configuration Management Tools	Although not strictly test tools, these are necessary for storage and version management of testware and related software especially when configuring more than one.
Continuous Integration Tools(D)	These tools are helpful in continuous build integration in agile practices. These tools are also commonly called as CI tools and used in combination of Continuous delivery (CD) tools.

Tool Support for Static Testing

Static testing tools are associated with the activities and benefits described in chapter 3. Examples of such tools include:

Tools that support reviews	These tools assist with review processes, checklists, review guidelines and are used to store and communicate review comments, reports on defects and effort. They can be of further help by providing aid for online reviews for large or geographically dispersed teams.
Static Analysis Tools (D)	These tools help developers and testers find defects prior to dynamic testing by providing support for enforcing coding standards (including secure coding), analysis of structures and dependencies.

Tool Support for Test Design and Implementation

Test design tools aid in the creation of maintainable work products in test design and implementation, including test cases, test procedures and test data. Examples of such tools include:

Test Design Tools	These tools are used to generate test inputs or executable tests and/or test oracles from requirements, graphical user interfaces, design models (state, data or object) or code.
Model Based Testing Tools	These tools are used to validate software models (e.g., physical data model (PDM) for a relational database), by enumerating inconsistencies and finding defects. These tools can often aid in generating some test cases based on the model.

Test Data Preparation Tools	Test data preparation tools manipulate databases, files or data transmissions to set up test data to be used during the execution of tests to ensure security through data anonymity.
ATDD & BDD Tools	These are Acceptance Test Driven Development (ATDD) and Behaviour Driven Development (BDD) tools which are common approach of agile methodology where tests are derived to meet the acceptance criteria and behaviour of the system.
TDD Tools(D)	This is another approach for agile methodology called Test Driven Development (TDD) where a test is written first without code and then the code will be written to pass the test

Tool Support for Test Execution and Logging

Many tools exist to support and enhance test execution and logging activities. Examples of these tools include:

Test Execution Tools	These tools enable tests to be executed automatically, or semi-automatically, using stored inputs and expected outcomes, through the use of a scripting language and usually provide a test log for each test run.
Coverage Tools (D)	These tools, through intrusive or non-intrusive means, measure the percentage of specific types of code structures that have been exercised (e.g., statements, branches or decisions, and module or function calls) by a set of tests.
Test Harnesses (D)	A unit test harness or framework facilitates the testing of components or parts of a system by simulating the environment in which that test object will run, through the provision of mock objects as stubs or drivers.
Unit Test Tools (D)	A unit test tool is used to perform unit testing on program/codes that are independently testable. These are performed using unit test frameworks.

Tool Support for Performance Measurement and Dynamic Analysis

Performance measurement and dynamic analysis tools are essential in supporting performance and load testing activities, as these activities cannot effectively be done manually. Examples of these tools include:

Performance Testing Tools	Performance testing tools monitor and report on how a system behaves under a variety of simulated usage conditions in terms of number of concurrent users, their ramp-up pattern, frequency and relative percentage of transactions.

Monitoring Tools	Monitoring tools continuously analyse, verify and report on usage of specific system resources, and give warnings of possible service problems.
Dynamic Analysis Tools (D)	Dynamic analysis tools find defects that are evident only when software is executing, such as time dependencies or memory leaks. They are typically used in component and component integration testing, and when testing middleware

Tool Support for Specialized Testing Needs

In addition to tools that support the general test process, there are many other tools that support more specific testing issues. Examples of these include tools that focus on:

Data Quality Assessment	Data quality assessment is to review and verify the data conversion and migration rules to ensure that the processed data is correct, complete and complies to a pre-defined context-specific standard.
Data Conversion and Migration	These tools, converts and migrates the data. This could be within a platform or cross platform as well, which is later assessed by data quality assessment tools.
Usability Testing	These tools are helpful in measuring the user friendliness of the application by following certain international standards based on the user group type. The user groups include, healthcare, banking, common users, etc.
Accessibility Testing	Accessibility testing is to test the ease of access to the differently abled users. Features related to that like, audio, brail engravation, etc will mapped to those of the international standards of these category.
Localization Testing	A localization tool is a specialized software that helps software developers, project managers, and translators to localize software, applications, documents, and other content.
Security Testing	These tools are helpful to identify vulnerabilities in applications easier & faster. They also meet compliance with security market standards & support all major programming languages.
Portability Testing	It is a process of testing with ease with which the software or product can be moved from one environment to another. It is measured in terms of maximum amount of effort required to transfer from one system to another system.

6.1.3. Benefits and Risk of Test Automation

Simply purchasing or leasing a tool does not guarantee success with that tool within a project or organization. Each type of tool may require additional effort to achieve real and lasting benefits. There are several pre-requisites before you can procure a tool and several steps required before rolling out a tool to full fledge implementation. There are potential benefits and opportunities with the use of tools in testing, but there are also risks involved in using a tool.

Potential Benefits of Using a Tool

- Reduction in repetitive manual work (e.g., running regression tests, environment set up/tear down tasks, re-entering the same test data, and checking against coding standards), thus saving time
- Greater consistency and repeatability (e.g., test data is created in a coherent manner, tests are executed by a tool in the same order with the same frequency, and tests are consistently derived from requirements)
- More objective assessment (e.g., static measures, coverage)
- Easier access to information about testing (e.g., statistics and graphs about test progress, defect rates and performance)

Potential Risk Involved in Using a Tool

- Expectations for the tool may be unrealistic (including functionality and ease of use)
- The time, cost and effort for the initial introduction of a tool may be under-estimated (including training and external expertise)
- The time and effort needed to achieve significant and continuing benefits from the tool may be under-estimated (including the need for changes in the test process and continuous improvement in the way the tool is used)
- The effort required to maintain the test assets generated by the tool may be under-estimated
- The tool may be relied on too much (seen as a replacement for test design or execution, or the use of automated testing where manual testing would be better)
- Version control of test assets may be neglected
- Relationships and interoperability issues between critical tools may be neglected, such as requirements management tools, configuration management tools, defect management tools and tools from multiple vendors
- The tool vendor may go out of business, retire the tool, or sell the tool to a different vendor
- The vendor may provide a poor response for support, upgrades, and defect fixes
- An open source project may be suspended
- A new platform or technology may not be supported by the tool
- There may be no clear ownership of the tool (e.g., for mentoring, updates, etc.)

It is crucial to understand and mitigate related risks before selecting a tool for given purpose. As tools are meant for specific activities in testing there are no disadvantages of a tool. A tool usage may result in no benefits if the risks associated are ignored.

6.1.4. Special Consideration for Test Execution and Test Management Tools

Test Execution Tools

Test execution tools execute test objects using automated test scripts. This type of tool often requires significant effort in order to achieve significant benefits.

Capturing tests by recording the actions of a manual tester seems attractive, but this approach does not scale to large numbers of automated test scripts. A captured script is a linear representation with specific data and actions as part of each script. This type of script may be unstable when unexpected events occur.

A **data-driven testing** approach, also a part of test automation frameworks, allows testers to prepare a test script which re-runs a single script with multiple set of data. It separates out the test inputs (the data), usually into a spreadsheet, and uses a more generic test script that can read the input data and execute the same test script with different data. Testers who are not familiar with the scripting language can then create the test data for these predefined scripts.

There are other techniques employed in data-driven techniques, where instead of hard-coded data combinations placed in a spreadsheet, data is generated using algorithms based on configurable parameters at run time and supplied to the application. For example, a tool may use an algorithm, which generates a random user-ID, and for repeatability in pattern, a seed is employed for controlling randomness.

In a **keyword-driven testing** approach, the spreadsheet contains keywords describing the actions to be taken (also called action words), and test data. This approach is quite common to execute random handpicked test cases out of a test suite. This approach is quite helpful when it comes to regression testing. Testers (even if they are not familiar with the scripting language) can then define tests using the keywords, which can be tailored to the application being tested.

Technical expertise in the scripting language is needed for all approaches (either by testers or by specialists in test automation).

Regardless of the scripting technique used, the expected results for each test need to be stored for later comparison.

Model-Based testing (MBT) tools enable a functional specification to be captured in the form of a model, such as an activity diagram. This task is generally performed by a system designer. The MBT tool interprets the model in order to create test case specifications which can then be saved in a test management tool and/or executed by a test execution tool

Test Management Tools

Test management tools need to interface with other tools or spreadsheets in order to produce useful information in a format that fits the needs of the organization. Test management tools often need to interface with other tools or spreadsheets for various reasons, including:

- To produce useful information in a format that fits the needs of the organization
- To maintain consistent traceability to requirements in a requirements management tool
- To link with test object version information in the configuration management tool

This is particularly important to consider when using an integrated tool (e.g., Application Lifecycle Management), which includes a test management module (and possibly a defect management system), as well as other modules (e.g., project schedule and budget information) that are used by different groups within an organization.

6.2. Effective Use of Tools

As discussed earlier, there are several steps to be considered before and after selecting a tool for the organisation in order to achieve continuous benefits and Return-On-Investment (ROI). We will now discuss the same in more details.

6.2.1. Main Principles for Tool Selection

The main considerations in selecting a tool for an organization include:

- Assessment of the maturity of the organization, its strengths and weaknesses
- Identification of opportunities for an improved test process supported by tools
- Understanding of the technologies used by the test object(s), in order to select a tool that is compatible with that technology
- The build and continuous integration tools already in use within the organization, in order to ensure tool compatibility and integration
- Evaluation of the tool against clear requirements and objective criteria
- Consideration of whether or not the tool is available for a free trial period (and for how long)
- Evaluation of the vendor (including training, support and commercial aspects) or support for noncommercial (e.g., open source) tools
- Identification of internal requirements for coaching and mentoring in the use of the tool
- Evaluation of training needs, considering the testing (and test automation) skills of those who will be working directly with the tool(s)
- Consideration of pros and cons of various licensing models (e.g., commercial or open source)
- Estimation of a cost-benefit ratio based on a concrete business case (if required)

As a final step, a proof-of-concept (POC) evaluation should be done to establish whether the tool performs effectively with the software under test and within the current infrastructure or, if necessary, to identify changes needed to that infrastructure to use the tool effectively. A POC is conducted to understand if the tool supports all major or necessary activities which currently an organization is looking forward to be supported by the tool. There could be more than one tool which can be considered for POC before selecting one for the organization.

6.2.2. Pilot Projects for Introducing a Tool into an Organisation

After completing the tool selection and a successful proof-of-concept, introducing the selected tool into an organization generally starts with a pilot project. A Pilot project means, an organization at any time may have several projects to kick-off or ongoing, just to avoid any unforeseen situations for all projects we always begin with the new tool being given to one project and ask them to use and share feedbacks on benefits achieved from real use. A Pilot project has the following objectives:

- Gaining in-depth knowledge about the tool, understanding both its strengths and weaknesses
- Evaluating how the tool fits with existing processes and practices, and determining what would need to change
- Deciding on standard ways of using, managing, storing, and maintaining the tool and the test assets (e.g., deciding on naming conventions for files and tests, selecting coding standards, creating libraries and defining the modularity of test suites)
- Assessing whether the benefits will be achieved at reasonable cost
- Understanding the metrics that you wish the tool to collect and report, and configuring the tool to ensure these metrics can be captured and reported

6.2.3. Success Factors for Tools

Once a Pilot project is complete, successful and reports that the tool supported the project with many benefits, there are several parameters which are required to be observed and considered before rolling the tool to rest of the projects. These considerations will also assist in gaining a continuous benefit from the use of the tool. Thus, success factors for evaluation, implementation, deployment, and on-going support of tools within an organization include:

- Rolling out the tool to the rest of the organization incrementally
- Adapting and improving processes to fit with the use of the tool
- Providing training, coaching, and mentoring for tool users
- Defining guidelines for the use of the tool (e.g., internal standards for automation)
- Implementing a way to gather usage information from the actual use of the tool
- Monitoring tool use and benefits
- Providing support to the users of a given tool
- Gathering lessons learned from all users

It is also important to ensure that the tool is technically and organizationally integrated into the software development lifecycle, which may involve separate organizations responsible for operations and/or third-party suppliers.

Quick Revision & Tips on Chapter 6

1. Benefits and risk of test tools are key area.
2. Must be able to classify and remember the tools within each category.
3. Special consideration for some specific tools includes additional info about test automation frameworks like, data driven testing and keyword driven testing.
4. Considerations before selecting a tool for the organisation understand the prerequisite.
5. Objectives of pilot project is quite often referred to ask a question from section 2.
6. Do remember the success factors for using a tool to complete your preparation on this chapter.
7. It's possible that you can expect one question using NOT or FALSE.
8. Quickly revise the bulleted point which would answer most of questions from this chapter.

This chapter will have 2 questions in the examination with following breakup

Chapter 6 Question Distribution	K-Level	Number of Questions per LO	Suggested Points per question	
FL-6.1.2 FL-6.1.3 FL-6.2.1 FL-6.2.2 FL-6.2.3	K1	Exactly ONE questions based on this set of 5 LOs is required.	1	**There is a total of 2 questions required for Chapter 6.** **K1 = 1** **K2 = 1** **K3 = 0** **Number of points for this chapter = 2**
FL-6.1.1	K2	Exactly ONE question based on this LO is required.	1	

 # For the exact topic number please refer the ISTQB® official syllabus.

Sample Questions on Chapter 6

1. **Some tools are geared more for developer use. For the 5 tools listed, which statement BEST details those for developers**
    i)   **Performance testing tools.**
    ii) **Coverage measurement tools.**
    iii) **Test comparators.**
    iv) **Dynamic analysis tools.**
    v)   **Incident management tools.**
    a)   i, iii. and iv. are more for developers.
    b)   ii. and iv. are more for developers.
    c)   ii, iii. and iv. are more for developers.
    d)   ii. and iii. are more for developers.

2. **A tool that supports traceability, recording of incidents or scheduling of tests is called:**
    a)   A dynamic analysis tool
    b)   A test execution tool
    c)   A debugging tool
    d)   A test management tool

3. **Which of the following is NOT a goal of a pilot project for tool evaluation?**
    a)   To evaluate how the tool fits with existing processes and practices
    b)   To determine use, management, storage, and maintenance of the tool and testware
    c)   To assess whether the benefits will be achieved at reasonable cost
    d)   To reduce the defect rate in the pilot project

4. **Which of the following tool can be used for change Management and version control?**
    a)   Functional automation tools
    b)   Performance testing tools
    c)   Configuration management tools
    d)   None of the above.

5. **Which of the following BEST describes a characteristic of a keyword-driven test execution tool?**
    a)   A table with test input data, action words, and expected results controls execution of the system under test
    b)   Actions of testers are automated using a script that is rerun several times.
    c)   Actions of testers are automated using a script that is run with several sets of test input data.
    d)   The ability to log test results, and compare them against the expected results stored in a text file

Answer to the questions can be found at the last page of the book

7.

Glossary

All Power is within You!!

8.

Mock Test

Instruction for mock tests:

- These mock tests should be taken as if you are writing a real exam to practice, passing criteria, time management, understanding the tricks involved.
- Make sure you have been through the reference book at least once before taking up the mock tests. As the improper preparation may lead to wrong answers and can bring down your moral.
- If possible, try listening to the video tutorials to brush up your learnings and gain quick tips with respect to answering the sample questions.
- While taking up mock tests please keep a stop watch next to you to keep a track on time of 60 min to answer the paper.
- The answers to the mock tests are provided separately at the end.

Mock Assessment 1

1. Which of the following provides the BEST description of a test case?
   a) A document specifying a sequence of actions for the execution of a test. Also known as test script or manual test script.
   b) A set of input values and expected results, with execution preconditions and execution postconditions, developed for a particular test condition.
   c) An attribute of a system specified by requirements documentation (for example reliability, usability or design constraints) that is executed in a test.
   d) An item or event of a system that could be verified by one or more test conditions, e.g., a function, transaction, feature, quality attribute, or structural element.
   Select ONE option.

2. Which of the following is a major objective of testing?
   a) To prevent defects.
   b) To validate the project plan works as required.
   c) To gain confidence in the development team.
   d) To make release decisions for the system under test.
   Select ONE option.

3. Which of the following is an example of a failure in a car cruise control system?
   a) The developer of the system forgot to rename variables after a cut-and-paste operation.
   b) Unnecessary code that sounds an alarm when reversing was included in the system.
   c) The system stops maintaining a set speed when the radio volume is increased or decreased.
   d) The design specification for the system wrongly states speeds in km/h.
   Select ONE option.

4. Which of the following is a defect rather than a root cause in a fitness tracker?
   a) Because he was unfamiliar with the domain of fitness training, the author of the requirements wrongly assumed that users wanted heartbeat in beats per hour.
   b) The tester of the smartphone interface had not been trained in state transition testing, so missed a major defect.
   c) An incorrect configuration variable implemented for the GPS function could cause location problems during daylight saving times.
   d) Because she had never worked on wearable devices before, the designer of the user interface misunderstood the effects of reflected sunlight.
   Select ONE option.

5. As a result of risk analysis, more testing is being directed to those areas of the system under test where initial testing found more defects than average.
   Which of the following testing principles is being applied?
   a) Beware of the pesticide paradox.
   b) Testing is context dependent.

c) Absence-of-errors is a fallacy.

d) Defects cluster together.

Select ONE option.

6. Given the following test activities and tasks:

A. Test design

B. Test implementation

C. Test execution

D. Test completion

1. Entering change requests for open defect reports

2. Identifying test data to support the test cases

3. Prioritizing test procedures and creating test data

4. Analyzing discrepancies to determine their cause

Which of the following BEST matches the activities with the tasks?

a) A-2, B-3, C-4, D-1

b) A-2, B-1, C-3, D-4

c) A-3, B-2, C-4, D-1

d) A-3, B-2, C-1, D-4

Select ONE option.

7. Which of the following BEST describes how value is added by maintaining traceability between the test basis and test artifacts?

a) Maintenance testing can be fully automated based on changes to the initial requirements.

b) It is possible to determine if a new test case has increased coverage of the requirements.

c) Test managers can identify which testers found the highest severity defects.

d) Areas that may be impacted by side-effects of a change can be targeted by confirmation testing.

Select ONE option.

8. Which of the following qualities is MORE likely to be found in a tester's mindset rather than in a developer's?

a) Experience on which to base their efforts.

b) Ability to see what might go wrong.

c) Good communication with team members.

d) Attention to detail.

Select ONE option.

9. Given the following statements about the relationships between software development activities and test activities in the software development lifecycle:

1. Each development activity should have a corresponding testing activity.

2. Reviewing should start as soon as final versions of documents become available.

3. The design and implementation of tests should start during the corresponding development. activity
4. Testing activities should start in the early stages of the software development lifecycle.

Which of the following CORRECTLY shows which are true and false?
a) True – 1, 2; False – 3, 4
b) True – 2, 3; False – 1, 2
c) True – 1, 2, 4; False – 3
d) True – 1, 4; False – 2, 3
Select ONE option.

10. Given that the testing being performed has the following attributes:
    *   based on interface specifications;
    *   focused on finding failures in communication;
    *   the test approach uses both functional and structural test types.

Which of the following test levels is MOST likely being performed?
a) Component integration testing.
b) Acceptance testing.
c) System testing.
d) Component testing.
Select ONE option.

11. Which of the following statements about test types and test levels is CORRECT?
a) Functional and non-functional testing can be performed at system and acceptance test levels, while white-box testing is restricted to component and integration testing.
b) Functional testing can be performed at any test level, while white-box testing is restricted to component testing.
c) It is possible to perform functional, non-functional and white-box testing at any test level.
d) Functional and non-functional testing can be performed at any test level, while Whitebox testing is restricted to component and integration testing.
Select ONE option.

12. Which of the following statements BEST compares the purposes of confirmation testing and regression testing?
a) The purpose of regression testing is to ensure that all previously run tests still work correctly, while the purpose of confirmation testing is to ensure that any fixes made to one part of the system have not adversely affected other parts.
b) The purpose of confirmation testing is to check that a previously found defect has been fixed, while the purpose of regression testing is to ensure that no other parts of the system have been adversely affected by the fix.
c) The purpose of regression testing is to ensure that any changes to one part of the system have not caused another part to fail, while the purpose of confirmation testing is to check that all previously run tests still provide the same results as before.

d) The purpose of confirmation testing is to confirm that changes to the system were made successfully, while the purpose of regression testing is to run tests that previously failed to ensure that they now work correctly.

Select ONE option.

13. Which of the following statements CORRECTLY describes a role of impact analysis in Maintenance Testing?

a) Impact analysis is used when deciding if a fix to a maintained system is worthwhile.

b) Impact analysis is used to identify how data should be migrated into the maintained system.

c) Impact analysis is used to decide which hot fixes are of most value to the user.

d) Impact analysis is used to determine the effectiveness of new maintenance test cases.

Select ONE option.

14. Which of the following statements CORRECTLY reflects the value of static testing?

a) By introducing reviews, we have found that both the quality of specifications and the time required for development and testing have increased.

b) Using static testing means we have better control and cheaper defect management due to the ease of removing defects later in the lifecycle.

c) Now that we require the use of static analysis, missed requirements have decreased and communication between testers and developers has improved.

d) Since we started using static analysis, we -find coding defects that might have not been found by performing only dynamic testing.

Select ONE option.

15. Which of the following sequences BEST shows the main activities of the work product review process?

a) Initiate review – Reviewer selection – Individual review – Issue communication and analysis – Rework

b) Planning & preparation – Overview meeting – Individual review – Fix– Report

c) Preparation – Issue Detection – Issue communication and analysis – Rework – Report

d) Plan – Initiate review – Individual review – Issue communication and analysis – Fix defects & report

Select ONE option.

16. Which of the following CORRECTLY matches the roles and responsibilities in a formal review?

a) Manager – Decides on the execution of reviews

b) Review Leader - Ensures effective running of review meetings

c) Scribe – Fixes defects in the work product under review

d) Moderator – Monitors ongoing cost-effectiveness

Select ONE option.

17. The reviews being used in your organization have the following attributes:

- There is a role of a scribe
- The purpose is to detect potential defects

- The review meeting is led by the author
- Reviewers find potential defects by individual review
- A review report is produced

Which of the following review types is MOST likely being used?

a) Informal Review

b) Walkthrough

c) Technical Review

d) Inspection

Select ONE option.

18. You have been asked to take part in a checklist-based review of the following excerpt from the requirements specification for a library system:

Librarians can:

1. Register new borrowers.

2. Return books from borrowers.

3. Accept fines from borrowers.

4. Add new books to the system with their ISBN, author and title.

5. Remove books from the system.

6. Get system responses within 5 seconds.

Borrowers can:

7. Borrow a maximum of 3 books at one time.

8. View the history of books they have borrowed/reserved.

9. Be fined for failing to return a book within 3 weeks.

10. Get system responses within 3 seconds.

11. Borrow a book at no cost for a maximum of 4 weeks.

12. Reserve books (if they are on-loan).

All users (librarians and borrowers):

13. Can search for books by ISBN, author, or title.

14. Can browse the system catalogue.

15. The system shall respond to user requests within 3 seconds.

16. The user interface shall be easy-to-use.

You have been assigned the checklist entry that requires you to review the specification for inconsistencies between individual requirements (i.e. conflicts between requirements).

Which of the following CORRECTLY identifies inconsistencies between pairs of requirements?

a) 6-10, 6-15, 7-12

b) 6-15, 9-11

c) 6-10, 6-15, 9-11

d) 6-15, 7-12

Select ONE option.

19. Which of the following provides the BEST description of exploratory testing?
    a) A testing practice in which an in-depth investigation of the background of the test object is used to identify potential weaknesses that are examined by test cases.
    b) An approach to testing whereby the testers dynamically designs and execute tests based on their knowledge, exploration of the test item and the results of previous tests.
    c) An approach to test design in which test activities are planned as uninterrupted sessions of test analysis and design, often used in conjunction with checklist-based testing.
    d) Testing based on the tester's experience, knowledge and intuition.
    Select ONE option.

20. Which of the following BEST matches the descriptions with the different categories of test techniques?
    1. Coverage is measured based on a selected structure of the test object.
    2. The processing within the test object is checked.
    3. Tests are based on defects' likelihood and their distribution.
    4. Deviations from the requirements are checked. 5. User stories are used as the test basis.

    Black - Black-box test techniques
    White - White-box test techniques
    Experience - Experience-based test techniques

    a) Black – 4, 5 White – 1, 2 Experience – 3
    b) Black – 3 White – 1, 2 Experience – 4, 5
    c) Black – 4 White – 1, 2 Experience – 3, 5
    d) Black – 1, 3, 5 White – 2 Experience – 4
    Select ONE option.

21. A fitness app measures the number of steps that are walked each day and provides feedback to encourage the user to keep fit.
    The feedback for different numbers of steps should be:

    Up to 1000 - Couch Potato!
    Above 1000, up to 2000 - Lazy Bones!
    Above 2000, up to 4000 - Getting There!
    Above 4000, up to 6000 - Not Bad!
    Above 6000 - Way to Go!

    Which of the following sets of test inputs would achieve the highest equivalence partition coverage?
    a) 0, 1000, 2000, 3000, 4000
    b) 1000, 2001, 4000, 4001, 6000
    c) 123, 2345, 3456, 4567, 5678
    d) 666, 999, 2222, 5555, 6666
    Select ONE option.

22. A daily radiation recorder for plants produces a sunshine score based on a combination of the number of hours a plant is exposed to the sun (below 3 hours, 3 to 6 hours or above 6 hours) and the average intensity of the sunshine (very low, low, medium, high).

    Given the following test cases:

	Hours	Intensity	Score
T1	1.5	v. low	10
T2	7.0	medium	60
T3	0.5	v. low	10

    What is the minimum number of additional test cases that are needed to ensure full coverage of all valid INPUT equivalence partitions?
    a) 1
    b) 2
    c) 3
    d) 4
    Select ONE option.

23. A smart home app measures the average temperature in the house over the previous week and provides feedback to the occupants on their environmental-friendliness based on this temperature.

    The feedback for different average temperature ranges (to the nearest °C) should be:

    Up to 10°C - Icy Cool!
    11°C to 15°C - Chilled Out!
    16°C to 19°C - Cool Man!
    20°C to 22°C - Too Warm!
    Above 22°C - Hot & Sweaty!

    Using two-point BVA, which of the following sets of test inputs provides the highest level of boundary coverage?
    a) 0°C, 11°C, 20°C, 22°C, 23°C
    b) 9°C, 15°C, 19°C, 23°C, 100°C
    c) 10°C, 16°C, 19°C, 22°C, 23°C
    d) 14°C, 15°C, 18°C, 19°C, 21°C, 22°C
    Select ONE option.

24. Decision table testing is being performed on a speeding fine system. Two test cases have already been generated for rules 1 and 4, which are shown below:

	Rules	R1	R4
Conditions	Speed > 50	T	F
	School Zone	T	F
Actions	$250 Fine	F	F
	Jail	T	F

Given the following additional test cases:

	Rules	DT1	DT2	DT3	DT4
Input	Speed	55	44	66	77
	School Zone	T	T	T	F
Expected Result	$250 Fine	F	F	F	T
	Jail	T	F	T	F

Which two of the additional test cases would achieve full coverage of the complete decision table (when combined with the test cases that have already been generated for rules 1 and 4)?

a) DT1, DT2

b) DT2, DT3

c) DT2, DT4

d) DT3, DT4

Select ONE option.

25. Given the following state model of a battery charger software:

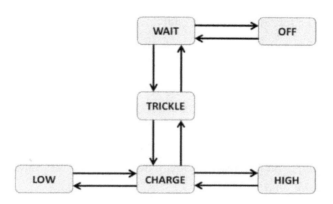

Which of the following sequences of transitions provides the highest level of transition coverage for the model?

a) OFF → WAIT → OFF → WAIT → TRICKLE → CHARGE → HIGH → CHARGE → LOW

b) WAIT → TRICKLE → WAIT → OFF → WAIT → TRICKLE → CHARGE → LOW → CHARGE

c) HIGH → CHARGE → LOW → CHARGE → TRICKLE → WAIT → TRICKLE → WAIT → TRICKLE

d) WAIT → TRICKLE → CHARGE → HIGH → CHARGE → TRICKLE → WAIT → OFF → WAIT

Select ONE option.

26. Which of the following statements BEST describes how test cases are derived from a use case?

a) Test cases are created to exercise defined basic, exceptional and error behaviors performed by the system under test in collaboration with actors.

b) Test cases are derived by identifying the components included in the use case and creating integration tests that exercise the interactions of these components.

c) Test cases are generated by analyzing the interactions of the actors with the system to ensure the user interfaces are easy to use.

d) Test cases are derived to exercise each of the decision points in the business process flows of the use case, to achieve 100% decision coverage of these flows.

Select ONE option.

27. Which of the following descriptions of statement coverage is CORRECT?
    a) Statement coverage is a measure of the number of lines of source code (minus comments) exercised by tests.
    b) Statement coverage is a measure of the proportion of executable statements in the source code exercised by tests.
    c) Statement coverage is a measure of the percentage of lines of source code exercised by tests.
    d) Statement coverage is a measure of the number of executable statements in the source code exercised by tests.
    Select ONE option.

28. Which of the following descriptions of decision coverage is CORRECT?
    a) Decision coverage is a measure of the percentage of possible paths through the source code exercised by tests.
    b) Decision coverage is a measure of the percentage of business flows through the component exercised by tests.
    c) Decision coverage is a measure of the 'if' statements in the code that are exercised with both the true and false outcomes.
    d) Decision coverage is a measure of the proportion of decision outcomes in the source code exercised by tests.
    Select ONE option.

29. Which of the following BEST describes the concept behind error guessing?
    a) Error guessing requires you to imagine you are the user of the test object and guess mistakes the user could make interacting with it.
    b) Error guessing involves using your personal experience of development and the mistakes you made as a developer.
    c) Error guessing involves using your knowledge and experience of defects found in the past and typical mistakes made by developers.
    d) Error guessing requires you to rapidly duplicate the development task to identify the sort of mistakes a developer might make.
    Select ONE option.

30. Which of the following BEST explains a benefit of independent testing?
    a) The use of an independent test team allows project management to assign responsibility for the quality of the final deliverable to the test team, so ensuring everyone is aware that quality is the test team's overall responsibility.
    b) If a test team external to the organization can be afforded, then there are distinct benefits in terms of this external team not being so easily swayed by the delivery concerns of project management and the need to meet strict delivery deadlines.
    c) An independent test team can work totally separately from the developers, need not be distracted with changing project requirements, and can restrict communication with the developers to defect reporting through the defect management system.

d) When specifications contain ambiguities and inconsistencies, assumptions are made on their interpretation, and an independent tester can be useful in questioning those assumptions and the interpretation made by the developer.

Select ONE option.

31. Which of the following tasks is MOST LIKELY to be performed by the test manager?
   a) Write test summary reports based on the information gathered during testing.
   b) Review tests developed by others.
   c) Create the detailed test execution schedule.
   d) Analyze, review, and assess requirements, specifications and models for testability.

   Select ONE option.

32. Given the following examples of entry and exit criteria:
   1. The original testing budget of $30,000 plus contingency of $7,000 has been spent.
   2. 96% of planned tests for the drawing package have been executed and the remaining tests are now out of scope.
   3. The trading performance test environment has been designed, set-up and verified.
   4. Current status is no outstanding critical defects and two high-priority ones.
   5. The autopilot design specifications have been reviewed and reworked. 6. The tax rate calculation component has passed unit testing.

   Which of the following BEST categorizes them as entry and exit criteria:
   a) Entry criteria – 5, 6 Exit criteria – 1, 2, 3, 4
   b) Entry criteria – 2, 3, 6 Exit criteria – 1, 4, 5
   c) Entry criteria – 1, 3 Exit criteria – 2, 4, 5, 6
   d) Entry criteria – 3, 5, 6 Exit criteria – 1, 2, 4

   Select ONE option.

33. Given the following priorities and dependencies for these test cases:

Test Case	Priority	Technical dependency on:	Logical dependency on:
TC1	High	TC4	
TC2	Low		
TC3	High		TC4
TC4	Medium		
TC5	Low		TC2
TC6	Medium	TC5	

   Which of the following test execution schedules BEST considers the priorities and technical and logical dependencies?
   a) TC1 – TC3 – TC4 – TC6 – TC2 – TC5
   b) TC4 – TC3 – TC1 – TC2 – TC5 – TC6
   c) TC4 – TC1 – TC3 – TC5 – TC6 – TC2
   d) TC4 – TC2 – TC5 – TC1 – TC3 – TC6

   Select ONE option.

34. Which of the following statements about test estimation approaches is CORRECT?
    a) With the metrics-based approach, the estimate is based on test measures from the project and so this estimate is only available after the testing starts.
    b) With the expert-based approach, a group of expert users identified by the client recommends the necessary testing budget.
    c) With the expert-based approach, the test managers responsible for the different testing activities predict the expected testing effort.
    d) With the metrics-based approach, an average of the testing costs recorded from several past projects is used as the testing budget.
    Select ONE option.

35. Which of the following BEST defines risk level?
    a) Risk level is calculated by adding together the probabilities of all problem situations and the financial harm that results from them.
    b) Risk level is estimated by multiplying the likelihood of a threat to the system by the chance that the threat will occur and will result in financial damage
    c) Risk level is determined by a combination of the probability of an undesirable event and the expected impact of that event.
    d) Risk level is the sum of all potential hazards to a system multiplied by the sum of all potential losses from that system.
    Select ONE option.

36. Which of the following is MOST likely to be an example of a PRODUCT risk?
    a) The expected security features may not be supported by the system architecture.
    b) The developers may not have time to fix all the defects found by the test team.
    c) The test cases may not provide full coverage of the specified requirements.
    d) The performance test environment may not be ready before the system is due for delivery.
    Select ONE option.

37. Which of the following is LEAST likely to be an example of product risk analysis CORRECTLY influencing the testing?
    a) The potential impact of security flaws has been identified as being particularly high, so security testing has been prioritized ahead of some other testing activities.
    b) Testing has found the quality of the network module to be higher than expected, so additional testing will now be performed in that area.
    c) The users had problems with the user interface of the previous system, so additional usability testing is planned for the replacement system.
    d) The time needed to load web pages is crucial to the success of the new website, so an expert in performance testing has been employed for this project.
    Select ONE option.

38. You are performing system testing of a train booking system and have found that occasionally the system reports that there are no available trains when you believe that there should be, based on the test cases you have run. You have provided the development manager with a summary of the defect and the version of the system you are testing. The developers recognize the urgency of the defect and are now waiting for you to provide more details so that they can fix it.

    Given the following pieces of information:
    1. Degree of impact (severity) of the defect.
    2. Identification of the test item.
    3. Details of the test environment.
    4. Urgency/priority to fix.
    5. Actual results.
    6. Reference to test case specification.

    Apart from the description of the defect, which includes a database dump and screenshots, which of the pieces of information would be MOST useful to include in the initial defect report?
    a) 1, 2, 6
    b) 1, 4, 5, 6
    c) 2, 3, 4, 5
    d) 3, 5, 6
    Select ONE option.

39. Given the following test activities and test tools:
    1. Performance measurement and dynamic analysis.
    2. Test execution and logging.
    3. Management of testing and testware.
    4. Test design.

    A. Requirements coverage tools.
    B. Dynamic analysis tools.
    C. Test data preparation tools.
    D. Defect management tools.

    Which of the following BEST matches the activities and tools?
    a) 1 – B, 2 – C, 3 – D, 4 – A
    b) 1 – B, 2 – A, 3 – C, 4 – D
    c) 1 – B, 2 – A, 3 – D, 4 – C
    d) 1 – A, 2 – B, 3 – D, 4 – C
    Select ONE option.

40. Which of the following is MOST likely to be used as a reason for using a pilot project to introduce a tool into an organization?

    a) The need to evaluate how the tool fits with existing processes and practices and determining what would need to change.

    b) The need to evaluate the test automation skills and training, mentoring and coaching needs of the testers who will use the tool.

    c) The need to evaluate whether the tool provides the required functionality and does not duplicate existing test tools.

    d) The need to evaluate the tool vendor in terms of the training and other support they provide.

    Select ONE option.

---XXXXX---

Mock Assessment 2

1. Which one of the following answers describes a test condition?
   a) An attribute of a component or system specified or implied by requirements documentation.
   b) An aspect of the test basis that is relevant to achieve specific test objectives.
   c) The degree to which a software product provides functions which meet stated and implied needs when the software is used under specified conditions.
   d) The percentage of all single condition outcomes that independently affect a decision outcome that have been exercised by a test suite.
   Select ONE option.

2. Which of the following statements is a valid objective for testing?
   a) The test should start as late as possible so that development had enough time to create a good product.
   b) To find as many failures as possible so that defects can be identified and corrected.
   c) To prove that all possible defects are identified.
   d) To prove that any remaining defects will not cause any failures.
   Select ONE option.

3. Which of the following statements correctly describes the difference between testing and debugging?
   a) Testing identifies the source of defects; debugging analyzes the defects and proposes prevention activities.
   b) Dynamic testing shows failures caused by defects; debugging finds, analyzes, and removes the causes of failures in the software.
   c) Testing removes defects; debugging identifies the causes of failures.
   d) Dynamic testing prevents the causes of failures; debugging removes the failures.
   Select ONE option.

4. Which one of the statements below describes the most common situation for a failure discovered during testing or in production?
   a) The product crashed when the user selected an option in a dialog box.
   b) The wrong version of a compiled source code file was included in the build.
   c) The computation algorithm used the wrong input variables.
   d) The developer misinterpreted the requirement for the algorithm.
   Select ONE option.

5. Mr. Test has been testing software applications on mobile devices for a period of 5 years. He has a wealth of experience in testing mobile applications and achieves better results in a shorter time than others. Over several months Mr. Test did not modify the existing automated test cases and did not create any new test cases. This leads to fewer and fewer defects being found by executing the tests. What principle of testing did Mr. Test not observe?
   a) Testing depends on the environment.
   b) Exhaustive testing is not possible.

c) Repeating of tests will not find new defects.

d) Defects cluster together.

Select ONE option.

6. In what way can testing be part of Quality Assurance?

a) It ensures that requirements are detailed enough.

b) It contributes to the achievement of quality in a variety of ways.

c) It ensures that standards in the organization are followed.

d) It measures the quality of software in terms of number of executed test cases.

Select ONE option.

7. Which of the following activities is part of the main activity "test analysis" in the test process?

a) Identifying any required infrastructure and tools.

b) Creating test suites from test scripts.

c) Analyzing lessons learned for process improvement.

d) Evaluating the test basis for testability.

Select ONE option.

8. Match the following test work products (1-4) with the right description (A-D).

1. Test suite.

2. Test case.

3. Test script.

4. Test charter.

A. A group of test scripts with a sequence of instructions.

B. A set of instructions for the execution of a test.

C. Contains expected results.

D. An instruction of test goals and possible test ideas on how to test.

a) 1A, 2C, 3B, 4D.

b) 1D, 2B, 3A, 4C.

c) 1A, 2C, 3D, 4B.

d) 1D, 2C, 3B, 4A.

Select ONE option.

9. How can white-box testing be applied during acceptance testing?

a) To check if large volumes of data can be transferred between integrated systems.

b) To check if all code statements and code decision paths have been executed.

c) To check if all work process flows have been covered.

d) To cover all web page navigations.

Select ONE option.

10. Which of the following statements comparing component testing and system testing is TRUE?
    a) Component testing verifies the functionality of software modules, program objects, and classes that are separately testable, whereas system testing verifies interfaces between components and interactions between different parts of the system.
    b) Test cases for component testing are usually derived from component specifications, design specifications, or data models, whereas test cases for system testing are usually derived from requirement specifications or use cases.
    c) Component testing only focuses on functional characteristics, whereas system testing focuses on functional and non-functional characteristics.
    d) Component testing is the responsibility of the testers, whereas system testing typically is the responsibility of the users of the system.
    Select ONE option.

11. Which one of the following is TRUE?
    a) The purpose of regression testing is to check if the correction has been successfully implemented, while the purpose of confirmation testing is to confirm that the correction has no side effects.
    b) The purpose of regression testing is to detect unintended side effects, while the purpose of confirmation testing is to check if the system is still working in a new environment.
    c) The purpose of regression testing is to detect unintended side effects, while the purpose of confirmation testing is to check if the original defect has been fixed.
    d) The purpose of regression testing is to check if the new functionality is working, while the purpose of confirmation testing is to check if the original defect has been fixed.
    Select ONE option.

12. Which one of the following is the BEST definition of an incremental development model?
    a) Defining requirements, designing software and testing are done in phases where in each phase a piece of the system is added.
    b) A phase in the development process should begins when the previous phase is complete.
    c) Testing is viewed as a separate phase which takes place after development has been completed.
    d) Testing is added to development as an increment.
    Select ONE option.

13. Which of the following should NOT be a trigger for maintenance testing?
    a) Decision to test the maintainability of the software.
    b) Decision to test the system after migration to a new operating platform.
    c) Decision to test if archived data is possible to be retrieved.
    d) Decision to test after "hot fixes".
    Select ONE option.

14. Which of the following options are roles in a formal review?
    a) Developer, Moderator, Review leader, Tester.
    b) Author, Moderator, Manager, Developer.

c) Author, Manager, Review leader, Designer.

d) Author, Moderator, Review leader, Scribe.

Select ONE option.

15. Which activities are carried out within the planning of a formal review?

a) Collection of metrics for the evaluation of the effectiveness of the review.

b) Answer any questions the participants may have.

c) Verification of input criteria for the review.

d) Evaluation of the review findings against the exit criteria.

Select ONE option.

16. Which of the review types below is the BEST option to choose when the review must follow a formal process based on rules and checklists?

a) Informal Review.

b) Technical Review.

c) Inspection.

d) Walkthrough.

Select ONE option.

17. Which of the following statements about static testing are MOST true?

a) Static testing is a cheap way to detect and remove defects.

b) Static testing makes dynamic testing more challenging.

c) Static testing makes it possible to find run-time problems early in the lifecycle.

d) When testing safety-critical system, static testing has less value because dynamic testing finds the defects better.

Select ONE option.

18. You will be invited to a review. The work product to be reviewed is a description of the in-house document creation process. The aim of the description is to present the work distribution between the different roles involved in the process in a way that can be clearly understood by everyone.

You will be invited to a checklist-based review. The checklist will also be sent to you. It includes the following points:

i. Is the person who performs the activity clearly identified for each activity?

ii. Is the entry criteria clearly defined for each activity?

iii. Is the exit criteria clearly defined for each activity?

iv. Are the supporting roles and their scope of work clearly defined for each activity?

In the following we show an excerpt of the work result to be reviewed, for which you should use the checklist above:

"After checking the customer documentation for completeness and correctness, the software architect creates the system specification. Once the software architect has completed the system specification, he invites testers and verifiers to the review. A checklist describes the scope of the review. Each invited reviewer creates review comments - if necessary - and concludes the review with an official review done-comment."

Which of the following statements about your review is correct?

a) Point ii) of the checklist has been violated because it is not clear which condition must be fulfilled in order to invite to the review.

b) You notice that in addition to the tester and the verifier, the validator must also be invited. Since this item is not part of your checklist, you do not create a corresponding comment.

c) Point iii) of the checklist has been violated as it is not clear what marks the review as completed.

d) Point i) of the checklist has been violated because it is not clear who is providing the checklist for the invitation to the review.

Select ONE option.

19. What is checklist-based testing?

a) A test technique in which tests are derived based on the tester's knowledge of past faults, or general knowledge of failures.

b) Procedure to derive and/or select test cases based on an analysis of the specification, either functional or non-functional, of a component or system without reference to its internal structure.

c) An experience-based test technique whereby the experienced tester uses a list of items to be noted, checked, or remembered, or a set of rules or criteria against which a product has to be verified.

d) An approach to testing where the testers dynamically design and execute tests based on their knowledge, exploration of the test item and the results of previous tests.

Select ONE option.

20. Which one of the following options is categorized as a black-box test technique?

a) A technique based on analysis of the architecture.

b) A technique checking that the test object is working according to the technical design.

c) A technique based on the knowledge of past faults, or general knowledge of failures.

d) A technique based on formal requirements.

Select ONE option.

21. The following statement refers to decision coverage:

"When the code contains only a single 'if' statement and no loops or CASE statements, and its execution is not nested within the test, any single test case we run will result in 50% decision coverage."

Which of the following statement is correct?

a) The statement is true. Any single test case provides 100% statement coverage and therefore 50% decision coverage.

b) The statement is true. Any single test case would cause the outcome of the "if" statement to be either true or false.

c) The statement is false. A single test case can only guarantee 25% decision coverage in this case.

d) The statement is false. The statement is too broad. It may be correct or not, depending on the tested software.

Select ONE option.

22. Which one of the following is the description of statement coverage?
    a) It is a metric, which is the percentage of test cases that have been executed.
    b) It is a metric, which is the percentage of statements in the source code that have been executed.
    c) It is a metric, which is the number of statements in the source code that have been executed by test cases that are passed.
    d) It is a metric, that gives a true/false confirmation if all statements are covered or not.
    Select ONE option.

23. Which statement about the relationship between statement coverage and decision coverage is true?
    a) 100% decision coverage also guarantees 100% statement coverage.
    b) 100% statement coverage also guarantees 100% decision coverage.
    c) 50% decision coverage also guarantees 50% statement coverage.
    d) Decision coverage can never reach 100%.
    Select ONE option.

24. For which of the following situations is explorative testing suitable?
    a) When time pressure requires speeding up the execution of tests already specified.
    b) When the system is developed incrementally and no test charter is available.
    c) When testers are available who have sufficient knowledge of similar applications and technologies.
    d) When an advanced knowledge of the system already exists and evidence is to be provided that it should be tested intensively.
    Select ONE option.

25. An employee's bonus is to be calculated. It cannot be negative, but it can be calculated down to zero. The bonus is based on the length of employment:
    • less than or equal to 2 years,
    • more than 2 years but less than 5 years,
    • 5 to 10 years inclusively or longer than 10 years.

    What is the minimum number of test cases required to cover all valid equivalence partitions for calculating the bonus?
    a) 3.
    b) 5.
    c) 2.
    d) 4.
    Select ONE option.

26. A speed control and reporting system has the following characteristics:
    If you drive 50 km/h or less, nothing will happen. If you drive faster than 50 km/h, but no more than 55 km/h, you will be warned. If you drive faster than 55 km/h but not more than 60 km/h, you will be fined. If you drive faster than 60 km/h, your driving license will be suspended.
    The speed in km/h is available to the system as an integer value.

Which would be the most likely set of values (km/h) identified by applying the boundary value analysis, where only the boundary values on the boundaries of the equivalence classes are relevant?

a) 0, 49, 50, 54, 59, 60.

b) 50, 55, 60.

c) 49, 50, 54, 55, 60, 62.

d) 50, 51, 55, 56, 60, 61.

Select ONE option.

27. A company's employees are paid bonuses if they work more than a year in the company and achieve a target which is individually agreed before.

These facts can be shown in a decision table:

Test-ID		T1	T2	T3	T4
Condition1	Employment for more than 1 year?	YES	NO	NO	YES
Condition2	Agreed target?	NO	NO	YES	YES
Condition3	Achieved target?	NO	NO	YES	YES
Action	Bonus payment	NO	NO	NO	NO

Which of the following test cases represents a situation that can happen in real life, and is missing in the above decision table?

a) Condition1 = YES, Condition2 = NO, Condition3 = YES, Action= NO

b) Condition1 = YES, Condition2 = YES, Condition3 = NO, Action= YES

c) Condition1 = NO, Condition2 = NO, Condition3 = YES, Action= NO

d) Condition1 = NO, Condition2 = YES, Condition3 = NO, Action= NO

Select ONE option.

28. Which of the following statements about the given state transition diagram and table of test cases is TRUE?

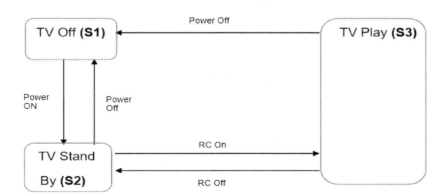

Test Case	1	2	3	4	5
Start State	S1	S2	S2	S3	S3
Input	Power On	Power Off	RC On	RC Off	Power Off
Expected Final State	S2	S1	S3	S2	S1

a) The given test cases cover both valid and invalid transitions in the state transition diagram.

b) The given test cases represent all possible valid transitions in the state transition diagram.

c) The given test cases represent some of the valid transitions in the state transition diagram.

d) The given test cases represent pairs of transitions in the state transition diagram.

Select ONE option.

29. A video application has the following requirement: The application shall allow playing a video on the following display resolution:

1. 640x480.

2. 1280x720.

3. 1600x1200.

4. 1920x1080.

Which of the following list of test cases is a result of applying the equivalence partitioning test technique to test this requirement?

a) Verify that the application can play a video on a display of size 1920x1080 (1 test case).

b) Verify that the application can play a video on a display of size 640x480 and 1920x1080 (2 test cases).

c) Verify that the application can play a video on each of the display sizes in the requirement (4 test cases).

d) Verify that the application can play a video on any one of the display sizes in the requirement (1 test case).

Select ONE option.

30. Which of the following statements BEST describes how tasks are divided between the test manager and the tester?

a) The test manager plans testing activities and chooses the standards to be followed, while the tester chooses the tools and set the tools usage guidelines.

b) The test manager plans and controls the testing activities, while the tester specifies the tests and decides on the test automation framework.

c) The test manager plans, monitors, and controls the testing activities, while the tester designs tests and decides on the release of the test object.

d) The test manager plans and organizes the testing and specifies the test cases, while the tester prioritizes and executes the tests.

Select ONE option.

31. Which of the following metrics would be MOST useful to monitor during test execution?
    a) Percentage of executed test cases.
    b) Average number of testers involved in the test execution.
    c) Coverage of requirements by source code.
    d) Percentage of test cases already created and reviewed.
    Select ONE option.

32. Which ONE of the following can affect and be part of the (initial) test planning?
    a) Test objectives.
    b) Test log.
    c) Failure rate.
    d) Use cases.
    Select ONE options.

33. Which of the following lists contains only typical exit criteria from testing?
    a) Reliability measures, test coverage, test cost, schedule and status about fixing errors and remaining risks.
    b) Reliability measures, test coverage, degree of tester's independence and product completeness.
    c) Reliability measures, test coverage, test cost, availability of test environment, time to market and product completeness.
    d) Time to market, remaining defects, tester qualification, availability of testable use cases, test coverage and test cost.
    Select ONE option.

34. Which one of the following is NOT included in a test summary report?
    a) Defining pass/fail criteria and objectives of testing.
    b) Deviations from the test approach.
    c) Measurements of actual progress against exit criteria.
    d) Evaluation of the quality of the test item.
    Select ONE option.

35. The project develops a "smart" heating thermostat. The control algorithms of the thermostat were modeled as Matlab/Simulink models and run on the internet connected server. The thermostat uses the specifications of the server to trigger the heating valves.
    The test manager has defined the following test strategy/approach in the test plan:

    1. The acceptance test for the whole system is executed as an experience-based test.
    2. The control algorithms on the server are tested during implementation using continuous integration.
    3. The functional test of the thermostat is performed as risk-based testing.
    4. The security tests of data / communication via the internet are executed together with external security experts.

What four common types of test strategies/approaches did the test manager implement in the test plan?

a) methodical, analytical, reactive and regression-averse.

b) analytical, model-based, consultative and reactive.

c) model-based, methodical, analytical and consultative.

d) regression-averse, consultative, reactive and methodical.

Select ONE option.

36. Which one of the following is the characteristic of a metrics-based approach for test estimation?

a) Budget which was used by a previous similar test project.

b) Overall experience collected in interviews with test managers.

c) Estimation of effort for test automation agreed in the test team.

d) Average of calculations collected from business experts.

Select ONE option.

37. As a test manager you are responsible for testing the following requirements:

R1 - Process anomalies

R2 - Synchronization

R3 - Approval

R4 - Problem solving

R5 - Financial data

R6 - Diagram data

R7 - Changes to the user profile

Notation: Logical requirement dependencies (A -> B means, that B depends on A):

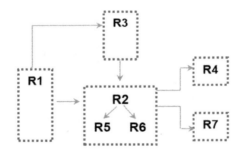

Which one of the following options structures the test execution schedule according to the requirement dependencies?

a) R1 -> R3 -> R4 -> R7 -> R2 -> R5 -> R6.

b) R1 -> R3 -> R2 -> R4 -> R7 -> R5 -> R6.

c) R1 -> R3 -> R2 -> R5 -> R6 -> R4 -> R7.

d) R1 -> R2 -> R5 -> R6 -> R3 -> R4 -> R7.

Select ONE option.

38. You are testing a new version of software for a coffee machine. The machine can prepare different types of coffee based on four categories. i.e., coffee size, sugar, milk, and syrup. The criteria are as follows:

• Coffee size (small, medium, large),

• Sugar (none, 1 unit, 2 units, 3 units, 4 units),

- Milk (yes or no),
- Coffee flavor syrup (no syrup, caramel, hazelnut, vanilla).

Now you are writing a defect report with the following information:

Title: Low coffee temperature.

Short summary: When you select coffee with milk, the time for preparing coffee is too long and the temperature of the beverage is too low (less than 40 °C)

Expected result: The temperature of coffee should be standard (about 75 °C).

Degree of risk: Medium

Priority: Normal

What valuable information was omitted in the above defect report?
a) The actual test results.
b) Data identifying the tested coffee machine.
c) Status of the defect.
d) Ideas for improving the test case.
Select ONE option.

39. Which one of the following is MOST likely to be a benefit of test execution tools?
    a) It is easy to create regression tests.
    b) It is easy to maintain version control of test assets.
    c) It is easy to design tests for security testing.
    d) It is easy to run regression tests.
    Select ONE option.

40. Which test tool (A-D) is characterized by the classification (1-4) below?
    1. Tool support for management of testing and testware.
    2. Tool support for static testing.
    3. Tool support for test execution and logging.
    4. Tool support for performance measurement and dynamic analysis.

    A. Coverage tools.
    B. Configuration management tools.
    C. Review tools.
    D. Monitoring tools.

    a) 1A, 2B, 3D, 4C.
    b) 1B, 2C, 3D, 4A.
    c) 1A, 2C, 3D, 4B.
    d) 1B, 2C, 3A, 4D.
    Select ONE option.

---xxxxx---

Answers

Answers for sample question on chapter 1

1. A
2. A
3. C
4. A
5. B
6. C
7. D
8. B
9. D
10. B

Answers for sample question on chapter 2

1. C
2. A
3. B
4. A
5. D
6. C
7. B
8. B
9. B
10. A

Answers for sample question on chapter 3

1. A
2. D
3. B
4. C
5. D
6. B
7. B
8. A
9. A
10. A

Answers for sample question on chapter 4

1. D
2. D
3. C
4. D
5. A
6. B
7. D
8. A
9. C
10. A

Answers for sample question on chapter 5

1. B
2. A
3. B
4. C
5. D
6. C
7. A
8. B
9. A
10. B

Answers for sample question on chapter 6

1. B
2. D
3. D
4. C
5. A

Answers for Mock Test 1

1.	B
2.	A
3.	C
4.	C
5.	D
6.	A
7.	B
8.	B
9.	D
10.	A
11.	B
12.	C
13.	A
14.	D
15.	D
16.	A
17.	B
18.	B
19.	B
20.	A
21.	D
22.	B
23.	C
24.	C
25.	D
26.	A
27.	B
28.	D
29.	C
30.	D
31.	A
32.	D
33.	B
34.	C
35.	C
36.	A
37.	B
38.	D
39.	C
40.	A

Answers for Mock Test 2

1.	B
2.	B
3.	B
4.	A
5.	C
6.	B
7.	D
8.	A
9.	C
10.	B
11.	C
12.	A
13.	A
14.	D
15.	C
16.	C
17.	A
18.	D
19.	C
20.	D
21.	B
22.	B
23.	A
24.	C
25.	D
26.	D
27.	D
28.	B
29.	C
30.	B
31.	A
32.	A
33.	A
34.	A
35.	B
36.	A
37.	C
38.	B
39.	D
40.	D

www.ingramcontent.com/pod-product-compliance
Lightning Source LLC
Chambersburg PA
CBHW081228050326
40690CB00013B/2692